How To Get Best Value From HR

How To Get Best Value From HR

The Shared Services Option

PETER REILLY and TONY WILLIAMS

GOWER

Published by
Gower Publishing Limited
Gower House
Croft Road
Aldershot
Hants GU11 3HR
England

Gower Publishing Company
Suite 420
101 Cherry Street
Burlington, VT 05401–4405
USA

British Library Cataloguing in Publication Data
Reilly, Peter A. (Peter Andrew), 1952-
    How to get the best value from HR: the shared services option
    1. Personnel management 2. Shared services (Management)
    I. Title II. Williams, Tony
    658.3

US Library of Congress Control Number: 2002104532

ISBN 978 0 566 08495 9

Reprinted 2007

Typeset in 9 point Stone Serif by IML Typographers, Birkenhead, Merseyside and printed in Great Britain by MPG Books Ltd, Bodmin, Cornwall.

Contents

List of figures and tables

Figures

Tables

List of abbreviations

ASP   application service providers
BPR   business process re-engineering
CEO   chief executive officer
CIB   Corporate and Institutional Banking
CIPD   Chartered Institute of Personnel Development
FTE   full-time equivalent
HR   human resources
HRIS   human resources information system
HSE   Health and Safety Executive
IES   Institute for Employment Studies
IT   information technology
IVR   interactive voice response
MBO   management buyout
MI   management information
NHS   National Health Service
OD   organization development
RBS   Royal Bank of Scotland
RBSG   Royal Bank of Scotland Group
SBU   strategic business unit
SLA   service level agreement
TUPE   Transfer of Undertakings (Protection of Employment)
USP   unique selling point

1 *What are HR shared services?*

The changing context

The human resource (HR) function has had a turbulent time over the last few years. In many organizations the pendulum has swung between downsizing and redundancy programmes and recruitment and retention difficulties. Organizations have increasingly paid attention to the customer, to the need for quality and cost improvement, to produce new products that stay one step ahead of the competition and so on. There have been new forms of service delivery. This may be a response to a more international operation or to a shift to the business unit as the primary organizational structure in place of the function. There may have been a tendency to decentralize responsibility for activities so that decisions are made closer to the customer or to re-centralize to emphasize the coherence of the organization. At an operational level, more and more work may be being completed in short-term project teams and less and less through traditional jobs.

The HR function has sought to respond and support this sort of organizational change, at the same time as finding its own role and contribution under scrutiny. Consequently, HR has spent considerable time examining itself, its role and its value in the light of the perceptions of it within the organization. This has led to changes in the way HR delivers its services. More work has been devolved to line managers. Activities previously carried out in house have been outsourced. The HR function has tried to become more customer friendly, more sensitive to quality and customer satisfaction. This may be reflected in opening hours, speed of response or the way technology has been harnessed. It has meant HR has had to spend more attention on the monitoring and evaluation of its performance.

Adding to the pressure on HR, whilst many businesses have claimed that people are their greatest asset, they have in practice often seen them as a source of cost not income generation. All too often this has meant that workforce numbers have been a soft target when cost reductions are required. This has placed demands on HR policies, practices and structures to react quickly to the changing business demands. It has made it more difficult for HR to pursue approaches that involve long-term investment in people and has encouraged a reactive response to problems that arise.

Cost reduction pressures have been at their greatest in what are deemed to be 'support' functions. As Alf Turner, then of BOC, said when explaining to a conference why shared services had been considered in his company: 'There is a relentless pressure on overhead costs that has consequential pressures on the cost of HR delivery' (Turner, 2000).

With increased devolution of people responsibilities to the line and administrative work outsourced or automated out, senior management in some organizations has started to question what value the function can add. If it cannot demonstrate its worth, then managers will wonder what the point of having an HR function is. Some leading HR managers believe that the function is now at a crossroads: either it has to show that it has a worthwhile contribution to make (through maximizing productivity or attracting and retaining the best talent) or it will find itself merely a contract manager of activities done by others.

It is in this context that the concept of shared services has emerged.

The concept of shared services

Like so many ideas, the shared services concept came out of the USA. It has not been seen as something peculiar to HR, but applicable to any form of service delivery. It has tended, though, to apply to services that support the primary operational activity. Thus shared service models have been created for finance, information technology, procurement, etc. So what distinguishes *shared* services from other forms of service provision? It has three key dimensions that in combination distinguish it from other models:

- The nature of the services provided is determined primarily by the customer.
- There is a common provision of services.
- These are available to a number of users.

The most significant of these points is that the 'user is the chooser' (Ulrich, 1995, p. 13) so that, unlike conventional internal service provision, the customer defines the level of the service and decides which services to take up. Thus the balance in the shared services model is shifted from producer to consumer. These services are on offer to whoever wishes to take them up; they are not restricted to particular groups. This is achieved by pooling the services for general use. Activities are therefore usually transferred from operating units to the shared services centre. This has been described as 'internal outsourcing'. It is important to note that *shared* and *common* provision of the service is not supposed to mean that it is *centralized* in the traditional sense of that term, i.e. that it is corporately determined. Rather, customer choice drives the model, the corporate part of the organization facilitates the process.

In practice, life is not as simple as this theory. In particular, some organizations may use the concept of shared services deliberately to centralize for reasons of cost cutting without having much regard to the customer. Nevertheless, in its pure form, the attraction of shared services is both this shift to reflect customer choice in line with business trends and the efficiency benefits that can be derived from concentrating dispersed services. In this book, we will concentrate on shared services in its pure form.

What parts of HR go into shared services?

Before looking in more detail at why organizations have opted for shared services, we need to put more flesh on the bones of the concept so that you have more idea about what is involved. We will use examples from organizations operating the shared services concept to give you a sense of the choices open to you.

Those organizations that have introduced shared services have included a variety of activities. To understand the options, we have categorized HR activity as shown in Figure 1.1. Organizations commonly distinguish between strategic, operational and administrative activities.

Strategic work generally includes setting the broad HR policy direction, aligning HR

Strategic	Policy
	Governance

Operational	Centres of excellence
	Relationship management
	Project work
	Consultancy

Support	Information and advice
	Administrative
	Record keeping

Figure 1.1　Categories of HR activity

Source: Reilly (1999)

activities with the business strategy and performing a governance function, i.e. ensuring that people in the organization abide by the rules of the game (e.g. in living the values). In our experience, such strategy work is always excluded from shared services model, as it is seen as a corporate responsibility and not to be shared with or determined by customers. This means that standards-setting and determining the values, mission and vision remain part of the corporate role to ensure that the organization follows the same broad approach to people management. The strategic role may well become the unique selling point (USP) of the internal HR function in the future – the area where it can add most value. Given its prime importance to the future of the function, it is right for you to keep control of this role and locate it at the centre of your activities. This is particularly true where substantial parts of HR have been outsourced, where employees are responsible for data-loading in e-HR systems or where devolvement to the line has removed much traditional HR work from the hands of the function.

Senior management issues (reward, development and succession) are also often treated as the preserve of the corporate centre. This is because of the sensitivity of the issues at stake and the need for high-level support. Moreover, dealing with external affairs, such as lobbying and participating in external bodies, is frequently kept as the responsibility of the corporate office. This combines well with the strategic work, emphasizing as it does the long-term and broader picture.

EXAMPLE 1.1

In one energy company, the corporate centre is very small and concentrates on HR strategy, management succession planning, external contacts and corporate governance.

At the other end of the spectrum, administrative and record-keeping tasks are the commonest elements to be included in the shared services function. The following items are often involved:

- recruitment administration
- relocation services
- payroll changes (on/off/variation – especially maternity leave)
- benefits administration (including flexible systems and share schemes)
- company car provision
- pensions administration
- employee welfare support
- training support and administration
- absence monitoring
- management information.

Not all these services are included in every shared service centre. Some are frequently outsourced (e.g. relocation services, pensions administration, training support and payroll particularly). This is where the work is deemed to be straightforward and where cost is a primary concern. Sometimes though, for example in training, external expertise is sought either because it is absent internally or too costly to maintain in house. Other services are not centrally located in a shared service, but placed closer to the activity they support. For example, recruitment administration is sometimes put with the recruitment team rather than with other administrative activities. The debate here is whether the benefit of economies of scale (by bringing things together in one place) outweigh or not the benefit of being aligned with those that are being supported (i.e. close to the action).

EXAMPLE 1.2

In 1995 a financial services company started their approach to shared services by combining the administrative support for one particular division. In 1996 they added the administration of recruitment services. In 1998, further divisions were added. This coincided with a major recruitment drive which, despite the throwing in of extra resources, compromised the performance of the personnel administration – recruitment work could not wait. So they decided to split recruitment out and return it to local HR units, since when the recruitment team has widened its service to include placing adverts and doing the first interview sift.

The provision of information and advice is another common feature of HR shared services provision. This can be provided via:

* written guidelines and procedures
* face-to-face contact
* an intranet to give details of personnel policies and procedures
* an email question and answer facility
* a telephone customer helpline to advise on the interpretation of these policies and procedures.

These sources of information serve different audiences and satisfy different needs. Some services (personnel guides in written form or accessible via the intranet) are offered to line managers so that they do not need to bother their HR colleagues with trivial or straightforward questions. Employees, too, can make use of these services for similar reasons. The helpline can also provide simple information or data, but it can go further. It can give line managers advice on the interpretation of HR policies. This might, for example, be on how to handle a particular disciplinary case or compassionate leave in unusual circumstances. HR colleagues may also use the helpline if there is particular expertise available.

EXAMPLE 1.3

BOC has a free phone line and anyone, managers or employees, can ask what they like. Pre-set options on the telephone system are:

1 pensions
2 payroll
3 share save
4 other HR query.

Calls are logged so that issues can be monitored; past history can be tracked and it allows charging on an itemized basis, if appropriate. One thousand two hundred calls were made in first month of operation.

EXAMPLE 1.4

Compaq's intranet is organized under the headings of:

• compensation and benefits – profit sharing, share purchase, flexible benefits, pensions
• payroll – tax and bank information
• training and development – including performance management
• employment – leave, equal opportunities, flexible working, maternity
• health, safety and security – accident report and occupational health
• resourcing – job opportunities, graduate recruitment.

The site contains 600 pages of information and is supported by a specialist adviser who looks for ways of improving the site.

Source: IDS, 2001.

Which of these options an organization chooses to offer depends upon cost (naturally the more channels the more expensive, but also inanimate methods are cheaper than those involving labour) and technological capability. More and more organizations are investing in computer systems and telephony to reduce the dependence on the more expensive human interaction. Some organizations though recognize that customers want different means of contact with HR so they offer the full range of communication channels. The expectation is that the intranet or written material will be scanned for factual information, that helplines or email will be used for giving advice or interpretation and that face-to-face meetings will be limited to the most sensitive or complex of situations.

EXAMPLE 1.5

An insurance company took the view when introducing shared services that they would offer multiple channels through which employees or managers could access HR. Thus people could contact by phone or email. They could look up a physical manual or surf their intranet. They could arrange to see HR staff face to face. The company did this despite realizing that having so many contact points was more expensive than having only electronic interaction. They hoped to wean colleagues off face-to-face meetings and off the phone and towards email and the intranet, but they recognized that not all staff would (yet) be comfortable with such an approach. Savings were made by aggregating disparate services. They did not need to make further savings by pushing people only to use computer-based interaction, especially if this risked giving shared services a bad name.

The greatest variation between organizations in defining the boundaries of shared services occurs in the operational middle of Figure 1.1. Nearly all large organizations have an HR person in a customer-facing role, variously described as a business partner or adviser, or relationship manager. They either report to a business unit line manager or to a senior HR manager, usually, but not always, separately from the shared services organization. This individual, or at most small team, is expected to support their line clients in terms of strategic development, organizational development and change management. This can be described as the transformational activities, to be contrasted with transactional administrative services undertaken by the shared service centre. Often they are expected to call upon the services of others. Administrative support comes from the shared service centre, project support from a consultancy pool and policy direction from the corporate centre. Business relationship managers then act as brokers, contracting these services in what in some organizations is a purchaser/provider demarcation.

EXAMPLE 1.6

The HR partners at BOC (IDS, 2001) are responsible for:

- giving direction on 'organizational issues, structure and strategy'
- providing leadership in implementation of HR policies and processes
- developing and managing service level agreements (SLAs) with the service provider
- work with corporate and other HR colleagues on developing HR solutions.

Many shared services operations have a project or consultancy pool. This provides a group of HR staff to tackle a wide variety of problems. These problems may be characterized by their complexity or time needed to deal with them over an extended period. So the consultants might tackle the design and introduction of a new performance management system. They might provide help in a downsizing and restructuring project. In some companies, customers 'hire' their consultant as they would a taxi – hailing the first available person. In others, consultants are grouped by business unit (so they have specific knowledge of its problems and people) or by professional subject area (e.g. reward or development). Having a segmented pool of consultants is less efficient in resourcing terms than having one group, but does allow individuals to build up knowledge of a particular field (necessary if they are expected to carry out complex assignments without internal or external support) or business activity (more essential in a heterogeneous type of organization).

EXAMPLE 1.7

In Shell UK Exploration and Production consultancy services are grouped around:

- reward systems
- resourcing and recruitment
- employee relations (including advice on employment legislation)
- learning and development (advice to managers and employees on learning strategies and methods)
- organization development
- business support (including process improvement and benchmarking support).

The consultants work in multidisciplinary groups appropriate to the assignment. They work in close co-operation with the HR 'Business Partners'.

The BBC's new corporate consultancy pool has 14 consultants available to the organization. They work on projects commissioned mainly by HR Business Partners where there is an identified business critical need or insufficient resource from within their HR operational team. This means they may have to handle high-priority work or projects that need especially sensitive handling. All are generalists, though with preferences or skills in particular areas. They are expected to be able to work in any business area and on any topic, but in practice, allocation of work is likely to be based on best fit in terms of skills/knowledge and the assignment, and on availability. Thought is being given to supplementing this internal resource with external associate consultants who might have specific expertise or could provide additional resource at peak times.

British Airways opted to have a general pool of consultants but then decided that their service would be improved if consultants were dedicated to particular businesses. The knowledge of individual businesses was found to be helpful.

BOC has what they call a 'professional services' group organized into four streams. These cover resourcing, training and development, employee relations and compensation and benefits.

Abbey National has a small team of senior HR Relationship Managers who work as strategic business partners with the business Executive Management teams. These relationship managers participate in the business planning processes and develop HR plans to deliver the business plans. They deliver the HR requirements by accessing the services of an HR Consultancy team and other functional specialists such as recruitment and training. The HR consultants typically manage business change projects working with cross-functional business teams and the HR functional experts. The HR consultants may also work as key contact for a business area supporting managers with smaller change projects and more complex individual employee issues such as long-term absence management and grievance and disciplinary cases.

Finally, there are the so called centres of excellence that give expert help in specialist areas. Commonly this would include reward and training and development, but might encompass organizational design or resourcing. In some organizations this expertise is located in the corporate office along with the work undertaken on policy direction. In other companies, it is part of shared services. The location of the activity depends upon the extent to which the organization sees it necessary to be customer responsive (and place it in the shared service centre) or more corporately integrative.

EXAMPLE 1.8

Unilever is about to launch HR shared services in the UK. It has three dimensions, as shown in Figure 1.2:

- self-service
- customer service
- centres of expertise,

all under the 'peoplelink' branding.

Its centre of expertise provides expert help and service to Business Unit HR managers. Its role is to:

- be accountable to clients for peoplelink service/delivery
- adapt service in line with business need
- share know-how and market best practice.

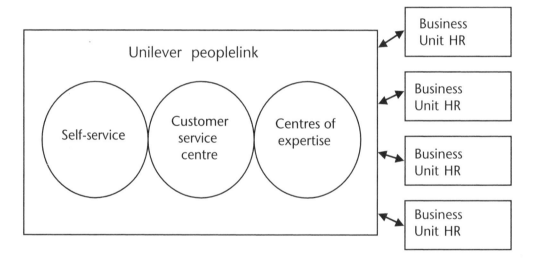

Figure 1.2   Unilever peoplelink: how the service will work

EXAMPLE 1.9

The Prudential Insurance company has eschewed the term 'centres of excellence' to avoid creating unhealthy expectations. Instead it has 'single provision centres' in its HR model. These are the owners of HR policies and processes. They employ specialists who are 'responsible for developing, enhancing and helping to execute business unit HR initiatives'. They act as consultants, advisers, coaches and troubleshooters for business unit HR staff.

For both the consultancy pool and the centres of excellence, in some organizations, guidance is provided to line managers directly; in others, these services are accessible by HR alone that contracts or uses them on behalf of their business partner.

The interrelation between the various elements of HR's activities is shown graphically in Figure 1.3 This is loosely based on the Prudential approach. It is generic in the sense that most of the elements are present in some form in big organizations, but the linkages may vary.

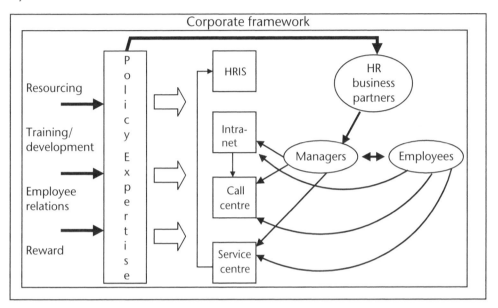

Figure 1.3   A model HR operation

Source: adapted from Prudential

To summarize, the experience of other organizations that have introduced shared services is that:

- Strategic work is kept at the corporate centre.
- Business relationships are best managed close to their business customers.
- Organizations can opt to have a pool of consultants or project staff in shared services operation to provide efficient resourcing. These people can act as a 'fire brigade' to deal with problems, can offer specialist expertise either on a business-specific basis or subject-expertise basis or to provide longer-term support to specific change programmes.
- Centres of excellence, defined by HR specialism, can be found in either the corporate centre or in a shared services model. Where they are located depends on the emphasis given to corporate cohesion or to customers, and upon the presence and role of the consultancy pool.
- Information and advice is usually a key element of shared services and can be delivered in a number of ways (personally, by telephone, by computer or through the written documents).
- Administrative tasks form the major part of any shared services model. However, parts may be outsourced or located with the activity they support.

Figure 1.1 can thus be annotated (see Figure 1.4) such that the location of the work can be specified on the basis of common practice. But how it would best look in your organization depends upon your needs and context. As the manager of HR shared services in one company put it:

> We are pragmatic about what is included in shared services. We do not make rigid distinctions between transactional and other work. We take an incremental approach, an organic approach, to the development of our services. This is especially true because we recognize that technological change will facilitate future options such that some solutions that look attractive now might look unnecessary later.

Nature of activity	Element of activity	Most common location
Strategic	Policy Governance	Corporate centre
Operational	Centres of excellence Relationship management Project work Consultancy	Corporate centre Business unit Shared services
Support	Information and advice Administrative Record keeping	Shared services

Figure 1.4   Categories of HR activity on the basis of common practice

2 *Why introduce HR shared services?*

So, having got a better idea of what shared services might entail, it is now important to understand in more detail why organizations choose to opt for this concept.

There are four principal reasons why organizations introduce an HR shared service. Because it offers:

- cost savings
- quality improvement
- organizational change
- technological development.

These reasons are sometimes discrete, e.g. shared services are introduced primarily to save money. Indeed, cost reduction is the most commonest reason cited by organizations for launching shared services. These drivers are also frequently seen in combination. So, even where cost saving is not the principal cause, it remains a significant feature of the decision-making process, often with a simultaneous desire for quality enhancement.

Cost reasons

Organizations believe that shared services can reduce costs by four main means:

1 cutting staff numbers
2 reducing accommodation charges
3 obtaining greater combined buying power
4 achieving greater efficiency in what is done and how it is done.

The first two benefits can be obtained by pulling together a number of separate administrative service activities into one place. This gives economies of scale. Headcount can be reduced by eliminating the duplication of activities. So instead of five personnel assistants around the country each entering data for their particular location, say, three can do it in one central location for the whole of the UK operation. The reduction in numbers comes partly from more efficient resourcing, especially in terms of absence cover. It also comes from converting more expensive activities and payroll charges to a lower cost base. So, for example, a telephone call centre may require fewer, less well paid people than found in the traditional HR team doing similar work. Using intranets is cheaper still in labour costs. Workforce reduction can also come from reducing the number of systems supported, be they technological or process. Percentage reductions claimed by organizations should always be treated with care, but headcount falling by some 20 to 40 per cent is the range normally reported.

EXAMPLE 2.1

In 1991 BT found that it had 46 bespoke IT systems, 30 different helplines and HR staff at 90 sites. Under its e-PeopleServe project, it has one HR Information System (HRIS), one helpline and three service centres. (IDS, 2000)

Standard Chartered Bank has offices around the globe. Many employ few people. By combining HR administration in one place (India) and introducing electronic services it expects to save £7 million per annum. This comes from cutting 130 jobs around the world and creating only 45 in the shared service centre. (Arkin, 2002)

Organizations can reduce accommodation costs by exiting from several offices, or by cutting room space. Further reductions can be achieved by relocating the shared service centre to lower-cost accommodation. For call centre provision this can be remote from customers, if so desired.

EXAMPLE 2.2

One media organization found different savings in different businesses. In one a 25 per cent reduction in staff numbers was obtained, but more through delayering than from the move to shared services itself. Another business did not cut staff but saved on office space by pulling people together. A third cut 20 posts because of economies of scale.

Economies of scale can also apply to service provision. Having only one or two central focal points to buy external services rather than a multiplicity is not just more efficient in internal resourcing, but also in using a common procurement approach. Centralizing buying power then can obtain a better price in the marketplace. Big savings have been made on recruitment selection placement fees, external recruitment advertising, car purchase, hiring agency temps or training provision. By using a restricted supplier list and offering the successful suppliers the high volumes of work that could come from company-wide coverage, charges to the organization can be slashed. Those organizations that have developed an internal market to service provision strive to use this as a means of driving down expenditure, especially where purchasers have the choice of buying services (recruitment, training, relocation, etc.) externally.

This means that HR professionals are having to develop contract management skills to make the most of their buying power. Their aim is to get the 'best bang for their buck' without unnecessary standardization.

EXAMPLE 2.3

ICL reported an annual saving of £2 million through centralizing recruitment services (Arkin, 1999) and reported at a recent conference that placement fees had by these means been cut by over 40 per cent.

Organizations achieve greater efficiency in their HR operations in a number of ways. This is sometimes done by streamlining the services on offer. Creating shared services allows organizations to decide to exit certain activities that are deemed to be non-essential or low value. Activities may be given up altogether or passed to a more appropriate person to do – often the line manager. Examples might be HR recording sickness absences or processing timesheets for overtime payment. Duplication of effort may be another reason to dispense with the task. Centralizing activities means avoiding the cost of supporting diversity and innovation, be it technological or process. This might be in having multiple reward or performance management systems across a company, often as variations on a theme. Or there may be multiple unlinked HR information systems that are separate from each other, each requiring support and connection, producing 'systems spaghetti'. Process improvements may be extended to reduce the amount of rework and checking that is done. 'Getting it right first time' can prove to be a money saver and can lead to further workforce reductions.

EXAMPLE 2.4

The Prudential discovered it had 47 forms of contract of employment with 250 variations. The HR shared services project manager asked: 'why?'

    Standard Chartered Bank had decentralized its management approach. HR support was in some offices organized around geography and in others around business streams. This tended to lead to a silo mentality, with much duplication of effort and spiralling costs. By combining HR administration in one place into a single shared service centre, the company was able to reduce expenditure, standardize processes and take advantage of new technology. (Arkin, 2002)

Automating processes is another cost saver that may be more easily achieved with a shared services setting than in a conventional structure, not least because the economies of scale of bringing activities together can fund the IT investment.

EXAMPLE 2.5

Shell UK Exploration and Production announced that to achieve their cost reduction and staff savings, it needed to:

- simplify its HR policies and transfer responsibility for adherence and implementation to line managers more than in the past
- streamline and automate HR processes, utilizing 'leading edge and cost-effective IT'
- exit from a number of activities, such as monitoring training budgets, making changes to personal data, facilitating salary or performance management reviews.

This would enable HR to continue to provide a high-quality service to the business, but with 'an increased focus on added value'.

Local government organizations under the pressure of Compulsory Competitive Tendering looked at new forms of HR provision. Some outsourcing took place for this very reason. Compulsory Competitive Tendering (CCT) has gone but it has been replaced by Best Value, and is having a similar influence, leading to reviews of internal versus external provision. In this context, shared services have been considered.

EXAMPLE 2.6

In 1997 Lincolnshire County Council began a process that anticipated Best Value by requiring each of its service directorates to review their performance and consider alternative delivery mechanisms. (IDS, 2000)

Kent County Council (KCC) reviewed the efficiency and effectiveness of its HR function in early 1999 under its own banner of Best Practice – a precursor to Best Value. The conclusion was that a full review was necessary in order to:

* revisit HR strategy in the light of changing business priorities, pressure points and external context
* recommend improvements to the way Personnel and Development operations are delivered
* clarify the cost of the delivery of these services.

The Best Value methodology was used to:

* challenge how things are done
* consult stakeholders
* compare how KCC performs in relation to other organizations
* compete with the market in terms of services delivered.

The outcome of the review was to improve HR's strategy, processes and structure.

Quality reasons

There are two strands to introducing shared services to improve the quality of the HR delivery. One is to work to higher quality standards per se and the other is to enhance customer satisfaction. From the standpoint of quality improvement, shared services can:

* make the HR function more professional in the work it does
* allow it to be more aware of best practice internally and externally
* achieve greater consistency and accuracy
* use better processes to complete its work
* deliver work on time and to budget.

Through these means HR can provide a more efficient and effective service. Through a greater self-awareness of the need to meet standards of service delivery, the HR function can achieve a more professional approach. This will be reflected in high quality performance. Human resource's work will be monitored in terms of accuracy and timeliness. It will be benchmarked against the best in class. Ideas for improvement can then be incorporated to make process improvements.

EXAMPLE 2.7

One financial services organization found when it undertook a review of HR procedures before it introduced shared services that there were a myriad of approaches which often led to inconsistency, which was particularly important to avoid where it affected legal, regulatory or corporate governance issues. The introduction of a shared services approach has led to a more consistent and rigorous approach in the application of regulated processes.

HR can also facilitate greater customer orientation in what it does through:

- being consumer not producer driven, i.e. to think of what the customer wants rather than what suits the service supplier
- becoming more accessible, e.g. by opening HR services for longer hours or by easing the means of getting in contact
- improving the supply of information to customers, both on process and content
- delivering more accountability, for example through formal service level agreements giving better quality support in line with customer needs
- operating user-friendly services.

As we will see, technology facilitates a number of these changes, but those introducing shared services are often seeking a change in attitude as well. A customer-focused approach requires satisfying customer requirements, not necessarily by adopting the traditional or the most convenient means, but by choosing the one that is most likely to deliver the goods. This suggests operating at a consistently higher standard and constantly seeking ways to improve. It also means delivering services in a way that is attuned to the needs of employees and line managers, be it in terms of time, place or manner.

EXAMPLE 2.8

At Powergen, the shared services manager put himself and his team through a Putting People First programme as his first action on taking charge. In their environment with most customers in the same building, the emphasis is on face-to-face contact. Getting these interactions right is the key to their success.

Of course, many of these changes can be obtained through other HR structures. The shared services approach has the advantage of bringing a wide range of activities in line with one another through working to a common template. Organizations can see benefits in pulling activities together in terms of commonality of information capture and learning. Change itself, of any kind, challenges the norms and allows the organization to alter attitudes as well as processes and structures.

Organizational reasons

There are four sets of organizational (i.e. structural) reasons we have seen behind the establishment of HR shared services.

PRODUCT OF WIDER ORGANIZATIONAL CHANGE

In some instances, shared services comes from HR responding to or participating in wider organizational change. This can be the result of a realignment of the way business is done. For example, regional structures might replace discrete national organizations. This has been particularly seen in the European context in line with greater European integration. Alternatively, structures may be grouped around business streams rather than defined by geography. Companies operating on a global basis may choose this route. HR structures will follow these changes and may lead to shared service centres based on the overall corporate configuration. Pulling together HR operations that were previously discrete may support the integration of business activities, be it on geographical or product lines.

EXAMPLE 2.9

In Shell International, the creation of Shell European Oil Products (SEOP) brought together all the 'downstream' companies of the region within a common organizational framework. This required a common cross-national business support mechanism, including HR. Shell People Services provides integrated services to SEOP, and many other businesses including such activities as recruitment, expatriate management and job evaluation, soon to be based on a common HR information system.

Devolvement of activities to line management may also necessitate a change in HR structure. This might be an HR initiated move or might be part of a general change in organizational philosophy. The transfer of responsibility to line managers may be sought in finance, logistics or HR. Managers may become expected to be more self-reliant and be able to take a wider range of decisions themselves. The reasoning here is usually to strip out bureaucracy and produce faster decision-making.

EXAMPLE 2.10

When in 1994 NatWest launched the model of an HR consultancy service and central services operation, it was done to improve service and quality delivery – and to cut costs. But it was also done to devolve more responsibility to line managers. The aim was to make HR less of an administrative function and more integrated with the business.

Conversely, the organization may be seeking a re-centralization of accountability, taking responsibilities away from devolved business units. Here it is not so much the line manager giving up power as a shift from subsidiary parts of the organization to the corporate centre. Bringing together HR activities spread around the organization into a central home may be one visible sign of re-centralization. The usual reason for this is to achieve cost savings and reduce duplication and unnecessary differences.

EXAMPLE 2.11

A high street bank started the move to shared services by centralizing payroll in 1994. Centralization was subsequently extended to the administration of employee benefits, training and recruitment. But its activities were still decentralized by comparison with another bank with which it subsequently merged. The latter worked to a more explicit centralization model that came from their chief executive officer (CEO). After the merger, the combined company adopted the more centralized view. The approach became:

1 to centralize services
2 to 'clean them up'
3 to re-engineer processes so as to improve them
4 to choose the most appropriate sourcing option.

Another cause of wider organizational change in this context is the introduction of a ubiquitous service culture, in which HR plays a part. Again cost saving may be a contributory benefit, but the reasoning behind the shift may have more to do with letting the operational side of the organization concentrate on its prime role. HR then is put in the position of a supplier to an almost separate business. This line of thinking encourages outsourcing (because of the institutionalized client/supplier split) and, to a lesser extent, combining all the support services into a single division to support the operational side of the business. It may also lead HR to organize itself by deliverables to the customer rather than by the more traditional functions.

EXAMPLE 2.12

Powergen's HR shared services is a £1.5 million and more business, employing up to 30 people, including payroll staff, plus seasonal contractors. It was established along with other 'professional' services to provide cost-effective activities in line with what the customer wants. The professional services are profit centres, earning money to cover their costs by charging out their work. The HR service reports to Services Division Director, with a dotted line to the HR Director.

Without going so far as to introduce a single service-based model for support functions, in some organizations one function has taken the lead in moving to a new model of service delivery. Others functions may then follow because the benefits of the new approach are so self-evident that all service functions examine how they can apply this learning to their own situation. We have seen examples where finance, information technology (IT) or HR has been the pathfinder.

EXAMPLE 2.13

In the NHS, the first investigation of shared services was to look at how the finance function across the whole service could be organized in a smaller number of centres (between 10 and 25) to repeat the benefits of economies of scale that new IT systems brought. This was further developed in local health systems by Primary Care Trusts so to avoid each of them setting up their own finance activity. Besides the economies of scale argument against the proliferation of finance departments, there was also the need to standardize systems and processes, both from a cost and good practice angle. This led to thinking about combining payroll and HR information systems. Further debate (and, in some cases, action) is now taking place about extending shared services to other aspects of HR.

ACHIEVING STRUCTURAL FLEXIBILITY

The shared service concept offers more structural flexibility. It makes HR 'future proof' against organizational reconfiguration. This means it is easier for HR to support customers during business change – clients might reconfigure their organizational structures but a common support centre can easily adjust. More fundamental change, such as from a merger or acquisition, can also be accommodated. Given the frequency of structural change it is hardly surprising that this is an aim from the shared services approach. Certainly, the shared services model is fairly robust in relation to internal change, as business units come and go. It helps when there is a merged operation, if the other company has a similar type of HR structure. However, if the HR models are very different, integration can still be problematic. Having said this, it is probably more likely that a newly formed company would opt for moving a traditional HR function to shared services than vice versa because of all the positive reasons we have reported (but especially the cost savings).

EXAMPLE 2.14

Abbey National moved to shared services not solely because of the usual cost and quality reasons, but also because it was felt that their existing structures were not sufficiently agile to support business transformation. It was recognized that frequent business changes would occur and that under the previous model this frequently necessitated HR organizational change too. This disruption impacted on the performance of HR and the delivery of HR solutions. The shared services model was chosen because it could better accommodate and be more responsive to alterations in business structures, enable knowledge and best practice to be transferred between consultants, and provide more opportunity for the HR consultants to gain broad-based experience.

BETTER ORGANIZATIONAL LEARNING

There is, it is believed by advocates of shared services, a benefit to be obtained from cross-company learning in this environment. By bringing services together in one place, there is the advantage that expertise is available for all, not just for a particular business. Good practice found in one operating unit can be made known to the whole organization. This can be a benefit of having a consultancy or project pool, if it is well managed. Centres of excellence may facilitate the same learning benefits.

Common information systems can be launched on the back of shared services, thereby improving access from different geographical parts of the organization, across the various functional or business groupings and potentially for HR staff, line managers and, even, employees. This is important when organizations are crying out for improved management information. Senior executives become very frustrated if they cannot be told about comparative sickness or retention rates across the organization, or even establish the number and type of employees. More accurate, timely and effective management information enables the HR community to gather evidence to support its interventions. This makes it more likely to add the very value it seeks to create and to deliver people-based policies and procedures that meet the organization's objectives.

EXAMPLE 2.15

One of the reasons why Telewest introduced shared services was 'to standardize and improve the flow of management information'. This includes absence, wastage and overtime statistics. Non-standard reports can also be produced. (IDS, 2001)

REPOSITIONING HR

Many companies use shared services quite explicitly to reposition HR and change its role. This means trying to help the function become more strategic and less bogged down in administrative activities. So the aim of HR has been to move from:

- a short-term to long-term orientation
- a purely operational to a more strategic role
- a reactive tendency to a more proactive orientation
- a policer of rules to an adviser to the line
- an upholder of tradition to a facilitator of change
- an employee welfare service to a business support function.

In other words, HR is seeking to avoid a low-profile, fire-fighting role and is wishing to become an explicit, high-profile contributor at the strategic level, well integrated with the business and demonstrably adding value.

EXAMPLE 2.16

Royal & SunAlliance is moving from being 'transaction dominated' through being 'process efficient' and 'functionally effective' to 'shaping and creating impact'. So, for example, HR will be involved less in the administration of remuneration or training, and more concerned with design.

Figure 2.1 shows the change in the direction of travel – moving up the arrow from short-term tactical to long-term strategic – whereas Figure 2.2 illustrates how organizations wish to rebalance the activities of the HR function to move away from administrative to strategic. It is the sort of graphic much used within organizations and by consultants to get the point across over where the concentration of work should be within HR. BOC, for example, used this picture to build the business case for change.

Figure 2.1 Change of HR direction

Source: Reilly (1999)

A move to shared services may assist the process. It is argued that this can be achieved by more clearly distinguishing between transactional and transformational services. Transactional work (administrative, record-keeping, information provision) can then be dealt with in the most efficient manner through shared services. Transformational activities (especially change and strategic management) can then be given the time and space to flourish through allowing both the corporate centre and HR business unit managers to concentrate on this type of work. If this is not done, it is said that administrative tasks tend to crowd out strategic change. Short-term, operational work tends to take precedence.

For this approach to be successful, however, it may need to be accompanied by other initiatives. Some organizations have achieved this through a concomitant devolution of personnel activities to line managers. This might involve routine administration (e.g. the recording of holidays or sickness), and the direct people management (e.g. discipline or welfare). At a more significant level, line managers have taken responsibility across a broad spectrum of activities, especially in recruitment and selection, employee relations, performance management and work organization.

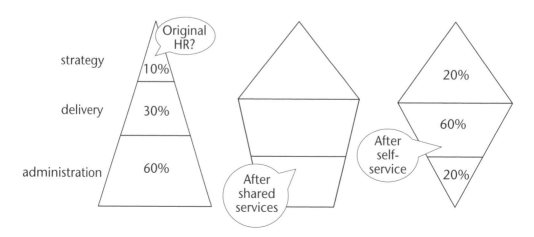

Figure 2.2 The changing nature of HR: the move from administration to strategy

Source: adapted from BOC

Tasks have also been shifted from HR to employees for them to carry out. This may be part of a conscious move towards creating a self-help culture for employees. This may be seen in employees inputting data directly into records systems rather than passing it to HR colleagues to do. We will describe this in more detail below.

Both managers and staff are thus expected to do more for themselves than in the past, and rely less on HR. This reduces the overall administrative burden on HR.

However, the power of new technologies to deliver timely and effective transactions to the line manager may challenge the traditional personnel role in many organizations. The function will be stripped of its *raison d'être* in a way that could see its decline in importance. This could be a decisive swing of the pendulum on people management tasks away from HR and to line management. It is for this reason that far-sighted HR leaders want to shift the HR role to that of the strategic player to avoid the trap of being an expert in administrative work that it no longer undertakes. This is a controversial topic, to which we will return in Chapter 9.

Technological facilitation

For some people, technology is regarded as a facilitator of change rather than a driver in itself. However, this may underestimate its impact. Some shared service models could not have been possible only a few years ago. Technical innovation in communications has enabled far reaching structural change to take place.

EXAMPLE 2.17

BOC (IDS, 2001) describes technology as 'essential' to the new HR model. This is because it:

- is a prerequisite to cost savings obtained through re-engineered processes
- provides the 'foundation for continuous improvement'
- integrates HR with the business
- creates a 'new breed of self-reliant managers and employees'
- offers accessible and consistent data and information
- standardized HR processes.

EXAMPLE 2.18

One innovation aspect of the new HR Operations at the BBC is the use of technology. As shown in Figure 2.3, a number of databases are linked together via a data warehouse. In practical terms it means that a staff member in Operations receiving a call from a customer (employee or manager) can instantly find personal details (grade, salary, etc.) from the SAP HRIS and look at records of previous interactions between the Operations centre and the employee. To answer any queries, the HR adviser can draw down information on for example company policy and forward it by email. A record detailing the conversation is kept. This allows tracking of the specific case (if it is not cleared on the first call) and subsequent monitoring and reporting of the type of calls received. This helps with understanding the distribution of their work and allows appropriate resourcing.

Other features of the technology model include knowledge sharing devices that permit members of a physically dispersed team to keep in touch with each other. Livelink creates a virtual community of users, able to chat, collaborate and access common information. This has the added benefit of controlling documents and processes so that you are assured of using the latest version of any policies or procedures.

The BBC took the self-conscious decision that, except during out of hours times, all incoming calls would be dealt with by a person, rather than use interactive voice response (IVR) technology to route calls.

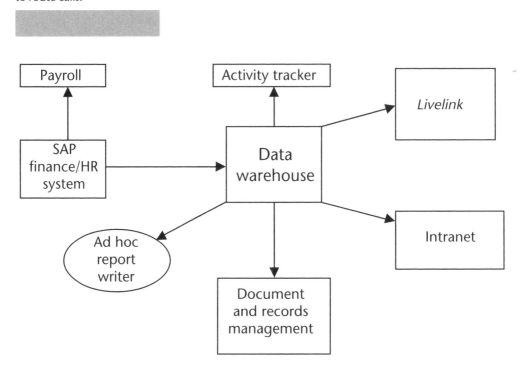

Figure 2.3   HR operations at the BBC: how technology works

Where technology has directly led change, it has occurred through the purchase of a new company-wide computer platform or a new HRIS. Either of these developments offers fresh possibilities in what can be achieved by data manipulation, or requires a rethink of how HR services are delivered. A common IT base allows the information networking that permits service innovation across the organization. Introducing a common records and payroll system can link data in a way not previously achieved. New functionality in an HRIS may allow the collection of skills' data or the holding of training records. Technology as an enabler of change comes from using such things as:

- an organizational intranet to provide information on HR policies and procedures
- PIN number based access to manipulate or update personal information, e.g. on options to flex individual reward packages, identify relocation assistance or lodge skills' data or a CV
- sophisticated telephony such as IVR to offer callers a choice of options to key into from a voice menu, or distributed call systems allowing callers to be routed to remote locations. This may underpin the call centre approach. This technology provides a better means to

ensure operational consistency is delivered in the application of HR policy through using tracking devices

- document management systems, e.g. allowing paper to be scanned so as to feed electronic files, to transfer material electronically and to permit multiple access by HR staff. This is particularly useful in recruitment where many documents arrive in hard copy and have to be both stored and sent to recruiting staff
- work flow systems that guide and prompt the user as to the next steps to be taken. It can indicate the point at which greater technical expertise should be mobilized. It can ensure that scanned correspondence is passed to the in-box of different technical specialists simultaneously, again speeding up responses. See Example 2.19
- standard forms on the intranet that can be electronically completed and dispatched to an administrative centre so that rekeying could be avoided. This might be training records or expense claims. Performance appraisal forms can also be downloaded and completed electronically. Applications can be made through this route to apply for internal job vacancies posted on an electronic bulletin board
- performance management and reward processes on line
- on-line training tools and access to learning packages and networks
- e-recruitment from vacancy requisition through applications on line to job offer
- on-line payslips
- the use of an 'extranet' that provides computer links to other service providers, e.g. employment lawyers or counsellors
- direct ordering of employee benefits, e.g. a company car.

EXAMPLE 2.19

Hewitt Associates, who run a number of benefit administration centres, use work flow to ensure that the front-line, first-level operators pass on more technical queries (on services such as pensions eligibility) to a professional expert using a simple 'Lotus Notes' type process. The operator will capture the essence of the query, the telephony system already has the callers' details preloaded onto the desktop, and the summary is then sent to the 'in-box' of designated technical specialist who will respond within preagreed timescales.

These developments are increasingly, but rather loosely, being referred to as e-HR. Technological innovation may be limited to operational improvement (automating or informing), but it may go further into self-service and allowing remote access or, further still, in transforming the role of HR – as implied in Alf Turner's statement reported earlier. In IT companies like IBM, technology is seen as being the building block of their service provision, as illustrated in Figure 2.4.

The aim is to provide an end to end process model (see also Figure 4.2 later) that starts with employee self-service and then moves to HR generalists, who provide first level problem solving and transaction processing. The next tier in the model provides functional specialists, offering a higher-level expertise in policy interpretation. The final tier is one policy design capability. (See Ashton, 2000, for a fuller account.) How much of these are really technologically dependent, apart from self-service, is perhaps open to question. In other organizations there is less need to emphasize technological support. Shell's on-line service is more typical of where organizations see the necessity of the IT contribution.

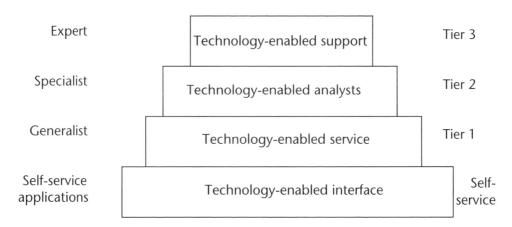

Figure 2.4   IBM's service centre process model

Source: Ashton (2000) © Business Intelligence. Reproduced with permission

EXAMPLE 2.20

Shell UK Exploration and Production is developing its HR Online service. It offers new, streamlined processes based on the principle that line managers and employees 'require simple, effective tools that will enable them to exercise greater control over the processes, enabling and embracing the concepts of "effective people management" and the "self-development culture"'. It means that activities can be done 'simpler, quicker and at lowest cost'. It provides access to personnel records and personnel policy documentation.

It enables employees to:

- view and update personal details on line
- access HR policies set out in an easy to read user-friendly way, at whatever time of day, and in a manner that makes it easy to operate (e.g. through search facilities)
- access other HR applications including the internal job advertising process
- provide links to third party suppliers of services or benefits.

It also enables line managers to:

- request changes to pay or benefits
- obtain management information on people matters
- keep up-to-date organigrams.

Siemens' vision of where they want to get to in future is not that dissimilar. Not all of the features shown in Figure 2.5 are yet up and running, but it is a help to have a sense of your ultimate ambition, not least to be able to justify the expense. One element – employee update of personal records – may not seem to be worth the investment itself, but being part of a holistic approach that transforms HR administration and the relationship with customers is perhaps a worthwhile prize.

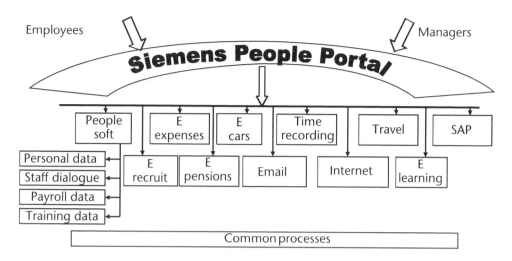

Figure 2.5   Siemens' future vision for e-HR (UK)

Introducing new technology is not an end itself. It enables the organization to complete work more efficiently through labour saving processes and more effectively by improving quality control. However, it is an expensive venture to upgrade computing and communication devices. It is estimated that the average cost of implementing self-service in the USA is $1 million (The Hunter Group Inc., 2000) and a UK employer found that to introduce an on-line pensions facility would itself cost £1 million. This has driven some organizations towards outsourcing (see page 31) because they cannot fund the capital investment themselves. Those that have got board approval for buying new technology may well have achieved this on the basis of making cost savings elsewhere, especially in workforce numbers. There is logic to this approach, but care has to be exercised in how this argument is deployed.

Conclusion

Cost drivers tend to predominate the decision to opt for shared services. There are those, however, where the desire to improve the quality of the HR service has been the prime reason. These two objectives do not have to be in conflict, but in some organizations they are. As we will see in Chapter 9, there can be a tension between efficiency through the standardization of processes, and improvement and choice in these processes. You can decide whether or not to use some or all of any cost savings to fund service improvement.

Whilst organizations may have primarily chosen to introduce shared services because it saves money or improves customer service, there are other benefits organizations report from this move. These are often a direct spin-off from the decisions taken. Having a more standardized approach to administration not only reduces errors but also provides more reliable management information. Better discipline in meeting customer needs through contracting and monitoring performance, leads to improved task and project management. If job rotation is practised, HR staff may broaden their skills and develop their careers.

EXAMPLE 2.21

In the Royal & SunAlliance HR review the aim was to:

- reinforce line managers' people management responsibilities
- position the function as more relevant to the business
- achieve these objectives at lower cost to the business.

To summarize, the advantages experienced by organizations opting for shared services are:

- lower costs, both in terms of numbers employed and accommodation required
- more efficient resourcing, within a bigger shared service centre pool than is possible if staff are distributed across a number of teams
- better quality of service, more consistent delivery to a higher, common standard. Non-compliance is more easily exposed
- customer satisfaction ratings increased, especially relating to those staff selected for their interpersonal skills
- improved match between customer expectations and service delivery, through more explicit contracting
- a single point of contact, making it easier for customers to access the HR function
- more of an integrated 'total solution' approach to a problem, rather than one fragmented by involvement of different HR disciplines
- greater transparency of costs making decisions on services better informed and more commercial
- more selective involvement by HR in what it does, so that it can have a greater impact. Time is given to issues of more strategic importance
- better project management – delivery is more likely to be on time and to specification
- the development of a wider expertise in covering a range of issues for HR consultants
- career development is facilitated by being able to rotate staff through different service streams
- cross-group learning within the shared service centre can be augmented
- the development of a cross-organization common information base, accessible to all
- better management information, provided more consistently across the organization as a whole
- the facilitation of corporate investment, especially in computing and communications infrastructure, where a bigger entity, like a shared service centre, can command resources in a way that smaller units cannot.

3 *The big design decisions*

Because shared services are introduced for different reasons and with much variation in content, how they are delivered similarly does not follow a single model. This chapter will describe the broad design options open to you before we detail the steps you should take to introduce shared services successfully.

Organizations have a number of choices. You can choose to have functionally separate services, one for HR, another for finance, etc., or you may opt for a common support provision. Then you have to decide whether to contract out these activities to third parties to undertake them on your behalf rather than carrying them out yourselves. If you keep them in house, you can choose to make them an arm's length entity, rather than integrate them with the rest of the organization. You can decide whether to physically locate your shared services centrally or opt for virtual integration of a dispersed operation. A key issue that will determine what you put in your shared services is how much you retain within HR and how much you devolve to the line or pass to employees under a *self-service* system. At a more detailed level there are questions to answer on the number of staff to be employed; whether the roles you create in a shared services structure are specialist or generalist in nature.

We will look at these issues in turn. Most companies will be introducing shared services in an existing organization; they will not have the benefit of a greenfield site. This adds constraints. These will vary from organization to organization, so the precise order in which you tackle the questions below will also vary.

Separate structures or common service provision?

In some organizations the shared services model has developed quite independent and separate functional provision. Each support function, HR, IT, finance, legal and so on has its own form of delivery. Several may use the shared services concept, but each delivers its own activities. In other organizations, there is a common support services structure within which each functional area operates. In a few organizations, integration has gone further so that there is a common access point or knowledge platform. So, for example, customers may ring a single phone number and then be routed through to the specific service they want. Or there may be a single database that HR, finance or IT people use, recognizing that some information is common to all.

EXAMPLE 3.1

IBM has a single telephone number to access the whole of its shared services centre. This covers HR, IT operations, financial administration, procurement administration and facilities management. Interactive voice response (IVR) facilities allow callers to direct their enquiries to the appropriate function.

You need to decide whether you want HR shared service to stand alone which has the advantage of being able to tailor your offering to meet your specific customer needs, or whether you choose a common platform with the benefit of shared costs.

Being clear as to the reason for setting up the shared services function (as laid out above) and the priority you have assigned to the factors should determine which is the more suitable approach. Put simply, tailoring delivers customer satisfaction and standardization delivers cost savings. This is a crucial choice. If quality and customer satisfaction are to the fore, then any savings made through headcount reduction or cheaper accommodation can be reinvested back into the services offered. If cost is the exclusive driver, and this leads to an emphasis on a common support platform, then it poses important questions on how effectively customer needs will be met.

EXAMPLE 3.2

A pubic sector organization had this dilemma. Do we introduce a single support organization that covers all functions? This offers the best savings and is likely to be most acceptable to senior management, but is likely to produce the most resistance from professional staff. Or, do we look for a model where improving the quality of HR is the principal driver and any cost savings are ploughed back into giving customer services a better offering?

To make or buy?

The most crucial choice to be made in the way in which shared services are delivered is whether to 'make or buy', i.e. whether to perform tasks internally or externally. Normally, external provision means getting an organization to manage and run an activity on your behalf. Specifically, with respect to technology, there is also the ASP option. This is discussed on page 34. Outsourcing is unlikely to apply to the whole HR activity. We know of no organization that has outsourced the whole of their HR function, nor seems likely to do so in the immediate future. The corporate role in particular, with its emphasis on strategy, policy-making and governance, would normally remain in house, as would those activities where organizational knowledge is especially vital. The exception to the latter point may be found in smaller firms. Here there may be insufficient expertise within the personnel function to offer managers a decent service, so outsourcing might be preferable.

WHAT IS OUTSOURCED?

Where, as is commonest, particular parts of the HR service are outsourced the following are the most frequently reported elements:

- payroll management
- employee records management
- training administration and/or delivery
- recruitment administration, search and initial selection
- pensions administration

- relocation and expatriate services
- occupational health, employee assistance/counselling/outplacement
- resourcing, especially of temporary staff
- benefits and salary administration.

As you will see it is the high-volume, routine, transactional activities that tend to be outsourced. It is easier to price this sort of work, set service levels and test the external market. Indeed, there are usually a number of potential suppliers that mean that competition will keep the price down. These activities are easily ring-fenced and capable of being allocated to another organization to perform on the client's behalf.

EXAMPLE 3.3

Abbey National has selectively outsourced a number of HR activities including pensions' administration and employee counselling.

Shell UK Exploration and Production contracted out relocation assistance and housing management.

Sainsbury's has contracted out its payroll operation for its 135 000 staff to RebusHR in an eight-year £20 million contract. Fifty staff will transfer from Sainsbury's to the contractor. The company expects to save money through the deal.

However, some organizations have gone further in their outsourcing extending it to the broader aspects of the shared service operation. So, for example, the management of the whole technological infrastructure might be contracted out – all the payroll, records, information and support systems, including the helpline and intranet. This might extend to consultancy services being offered by a third party.

EXAMPLE 3.4

BP has made a clear decision to retain strategy, policy, employee development and legal/regulatory matters in house, but to outsource the administration, implementation and delivery of HR services. By way of illustration, on compensation BP determines the strategy, designs the programmes and policies. Exult (the contract provider) conducts remuneration surveys, documents and administers pay changes.

Westminster City Council has kept an in-house team of 11 staff to be responsible for strategic and policy development, corporate employee relations, senior-level recruitment, advice to chief officers and elected members and contract management. Capita supplies other services defined as recruitment, operational personnel, training administration and co-ordination. (IDS, 2000)

REASONS TO OUTSOURCE

Why might you outsource part or all of your operation? The reasons other organizations give are that it helps to:

- save costs. Outsourcing shared services to a third party provider can achieve economies of scale. This will be true if you are from a small or medium-sized organization that can use the size of the supplier to achieve cost reductions similar to those enjoyed by large companies combining activities internally. This may be done because the supplier can offer services to a number of organizations from the same base
- switch from fixed to variable costs. This has advantages where there is pressure to reduce fixed costs, but where operating expenditure is under less pressure
- improve the service by using a specialist supplier that has specific expertise. This may be particularly relevant where the contractor has technological expertise to set up an intranet or call centre. Again if you are a small company you might also seek to obtain your general HR advice or employment law expertise externally
- free up managerial time to focus on core business issues. Management sometimes finds itself talking too much about the daily trivia and too little about the big issues. Outsourcing can be seen as a means of getting someone else to worry about everyday crises
- give greater flexibility in meeting fluctuating work demand. For work with a high demand variability, say recruitment, and sometimes training, having work outsourced means that the supplier has to worry about staffing arrangements. The bigger the contractor the more likely they are to successfully achieve this resourcing flexibility
- offer a new, extended, service model. Outsourcing shared services may be felt to be necessary where there is a need to operate cross-nationally and for services to be available 24 hours a day, seven days a week. An external service provider may be able to offer such a service if itself is a multinational operating worldwide. By comparison your organization might not be geared up to offer such a service, perhaps because it is difficult to offer non-standard hours working within the culture of your organization
- reduce exposure to regulations, legislation, etc. Again, small companies may benefit from calling on the expertise of others to help them through the complexity of changing employment law. An active government can generate a lot of new legislation. Think of the minimum wage, parental leave, working time regulations and part-time rights – just some of the changes in recent years
- obtain and keep staff. Employee turnover and an inability to recruit suitable staff can be another contributory factor to outsourcing. This may be especially valid in a tight labour market but can also be true if the contractor has a reputation that allows it to attract and retain good quality staff in a way that your organization does not. Information technology is often one such area
- reduce headcount (if not necessarily costs). Most outsourcing deals involve the transfer of staff from client to contractor. Those managers faced with having to cut staff numbers may see outsourcing as a relatively painless way of achieving this objective. Given that Transfer of Undertakings legislation more or less ensures that the terms and conditions of the transferring employees are retained (at least initially), then there may not be cost savings to be obtained unless the contractor can perform the tasks with fewer people
- effect cultural change. This may have multiple dimensions. It may be used as a general catalyst for change in attitudes and behaviour. It might encourage staff to be more commercial in their thinking. Using the discipline of working to contracts, rather than relying upon internal management accountabilities, may bring a more cost-conscious way of working.

Cost, quality improvement and achieving focus are the most important items on this list.

This is borne out by recent research (WERS, 1998) that found that 45 per cent of firms outsourced to save money, 20 per cent to improve services and a similar figure aimed to focus on core activities.

You may favour full outsourcing, or at least the technically demanding parts, where there are high investment costs. Thus organizations that need to invest heavily in their IT infrastructure are more likely to look outside for help. Even the biggest organizations may not be able to afford or justify the spending upon the new interactive technology, and outsource as a consequence. This is because it may be easier to absorb the annual charge by a contractor on operating costs, than a one-off capital charge. Moreover, some organizations fear that they do not have the skills to manage a high-cost, technically complex project and would prefer external experts to take responsibility. Outsourcing may also be chosen as a short–medium term 'fix' whilst e-HR processes and other technologies develop. This allows organizations to leapfrog to more radical service options, not being forced to invest in interim arrangements that create an internal legacy that has to be scrapped before it can deliver a payback.

Outsourcing is also likely to appeal to those of you in small or medium-sized companies that:

- cannot justify the investment in HR expertise in house
- can obtain economies of scale through buying into a common service provision
- are unable to attract or retain the right quality of HR staff
- are attracted to the notion that it is better for an external expert to worry about the latest employment legislation or options in family-friendly working.

The upside of this approach is that you can obtain an HR service not usually open to you because your size does not permit it. The downside is that the quid pro quo of combined provision offered by outsourcers is that you have to accept a largely standardized service delivery, with perhaps some limited bespoke items, rather than being able to create your own tailor-made service.

Larger organizations may seek cost savings by exploiting the external market (as in payroll processing) and/or want to pass responsibility to those specializing in a particular field (such as recruitment, training or relocation). Such organizations may believe that there are further savings to be achieved by combining with others through using a specialist contractor, especially on a global basis.

PROBLEMS WITH OUTSOURCING

Despite these reasons to proceed with outsourcing, it has not been without its difficulties. There have been problems associated with both the transition to outsourcing (such as employee relations difficulties borne out of employee objections to the transfer itself or its terms) and its operation (e.g. issues concerning the contractual definition of the tasks that need to be performed). Some of the problems surface early on; others appear when you want to change the nature of the contract, but are inhibited by either the contract itself or the way in which the supplier chooses to respond.

EXAMPLE 3.5

One transport company outsourced its recruitment administration to a third party provider. It was a very successful move. Costs fell and quality standards were maintained. The company decided, therefore, to extend outsourcing into recruitment selection. Because of its success the firm doing the recruitment administration was asked to extend its role, despite the absence of a track record in selection interviewing. The contractor had to recruit extra staff to do the work. The result was disastrous. The quality of decision-making by the contractor's employees was poor. The transport company cancelled the selection contract and brought the work back in house.

Some of the above problems with outsourcing have stemmed from the basis upon which the decision was made. Unfortunately, organizations have been tempted to outsource problem activities. 'We can't run them effectively, so we will get another lot to do it' is the argument. Contractors charge a great deal of money to sort out your problems. On other occasions outsourcing has been done to follow the latest fad or fashion without due consideration of the implications. In the public sector especially, some outsourcing has been ideologically driven: it is a good thing in itself, irrespective of the specific costs or benefits.

Against this background there are organizations that take the view that it is better to carry out tasks in house. This may be because they cannot believe that an external provider will be able more cheaply than themselves to undertake the work to the same quality standard and make a profit. Some organizations want to have control over all their processes or are not tempted by the alleged cost savings. They may believe that there is a fundamental difference of outlook between the contractor (wishing to maximize profit) and the client (aiming to minimize cost), which means that contractors will try to exploit the contract to their benefit. Ultimately, it is not the contractor that has the responsibility for the integrity of the service but the organization itself. For other managers, they think their circumstances are unique and would not be adequately carried out by an organization ignorant of the culture, processes and systems of the organization.

EXAMPLE 3.6

A Shell manager at a recent conference explained why Shell People Services had chosen not to outsource its activities:

- The importance given to internal knowledge.
- The ability to develop and circulate staff between shared services and its customers.
- All staff providing services are aligned toward the success of the whole enterprise.
- Any benefits from their operation (be they financial, intellectual or service) stayed within the company.
- Suppliers and customers being part of the same organization allowed for more 'customer intimacy' on the part of the service deliverers.
- Their operation acted as a 'gateway' to the outside world: they were not part of it.

The former HR shared services manager at Powergen explained that they had reviewed outsourcing their payroll, but decided not to outsource. They wanted an integrated payroll/HRIS and had not found it to be cost-effective to get external provision. They felt the system was too complex and too subject to change. They wanted flexibility, but this cost money if outsourced.

A media company chose not to consider outsourcing because:

- it had had a difficult experience over outsourcing financial services
- it believed there was no longer a cost benefit because Transfer of Undertakings (Protection of Employment) regulations (TUPE) meant that payroll costs could not be reduced by much
- it recognized that problems should not be outsourced; any that existed should be resolved internally
- managing activities in house meant that HR was in the driving seat, not pushed by anyone else to take decisions they might not want to take.

CONTRACTUAL PARTNERSHIPS AND CO-SOURCING

Partly as a response to the above criticisms, especially that contractors will exploit the contractual relationship to their advantage, some organizations have chosen to enter a *partnership deal* with their supplier. This emphasizes the mutuality of the relationship – the fact that both parties are reliant on each other for success, and risks and rewards are shared.

EXAMPLE 3.7

Lincolnshire County Council concluded a 10-year partnership deal with Hyder Business Services. Hyder's bid was explicitly for a partnership arrangement that offered not just savings to the council but also investment in IT systems. It stressed its own public sector background that it thought would complement the county council's own public service ethos. (IDS, 2000)

One organization has gone further such that the client is borrowing money from their IT service provider in order to invest in e-HR, the IT support for which will come from the contractor.

Thus organizations contemplating outsourcing have a choice between entering into a partnership relationship with their supplier or concluding a purely transactional deal. If you have complex or business critical services, you are likely to choose a partnership arrangement. Here quality improvement will probably be the main goal rather than cost savings. If, alternatively, your principal aim is to deliver cost reduction then a transactional deal might work best. In these circumstances short contracts should be used with services that are relatively easy to define and manage, and where the process is easily bounded. For example, training or recruitment administration are suitable candidates for short-term, cost-driven deals; whereas, support in, say, organizational development would be better over a longer period in a partnership type of contract.

Some organizations have gone further than partnerships with their contractors to create joint ventures with their service providers to allow both parties to fully benefit from the arrangement. See Example 3.8.

EXAMPLE 3.8

BAE Systems is setting up a joint venture with Xchanging (an Internet company). As planned, the proposal is to transfer 460 staff from BAE Systems to the new company to be called Togethr HR. It will support BAE Systems and subsequently, it is hoped, sell its services to others. BAE Systems benefits by taking advantage of the technological expertise of Xchanging and its investment in e-HR, and from the continuity of transferring its own staff into what it expects to be a long-term arrangement and from half the profits that should accrue once the new venture sells externally. (IDS, 2000; Hammond 2001)

Another variation of outsourcing HR services is the emergence of co-sourcing. Here the idea is to recognize that there is no such thing as a discrete HR process that can easily be hived off as a separate activity to an external supplier. Rather, there are integrated processes where part of the process or service can be provided by the contractor and part by the client. Thus, for example, there are many stages in recruitment from acknowledging there is a vacancy, through advertising, selection to induction. Some of these processes, such as advertising, may be done externally by one organization, recruitment administration may be done by another contractor and other parts, say selection and induction, by the recruiting organization. Co-sourcing aims to join these activities together, to minimize the process 'hand-offs' between the internal and external relationships. This is particularly important where organizations outsource part of their function – e.g. the back office administration or front office call centre – but retain the other half. This has the advantage that errors that appear in one place (say payroll) can be tracked to their cause (e.g. in recruitment).

With this in mind, outsourcing becomes not a way of separating out services to be executed by different organizations, but a means of joining providers together. So partnership in this case is not just about sharing profits or benefiting from savings, it is about understanding the contribution of all to the service delivery in an integrated manner.

An example of co-sourcing can be found in the Royal Bank of Scotland Group case study in Chapter 8.

ASP solutions

Application service providers (ASPs) are common in the USA and are growing in number in the UK. Application service providers are agents that assemble functionality required by organizations. This might be software applications, data storage or reporting tools. These are packaged with other services, including outsourced services. Access to the applications is normally through a standard web browser. Instead of buying systems software, the user usually pays a monthly fee to the supplier to cover service, support and development.

EXAMPLE 3.9

Siemens UK, for example, uses an ASP for their e-recruitment process. Thus recruitment managers who access the e-recruitment facility are in fact connecting, not with Siemens' in-house server, but with the server of the ASP.

The key difference compared with outsourcing is that ASPs act remotely rather than on a customer site and applications are leased over a network. You control the data input and management.

Its advantages are that:

- organizations do not need in-house IT expertise to set up and run their system
- set up time is very quick and few items of equipment are necessary
- capital outlay is also minimal. Like outsourcing costs are transferred from capital to operating expenditure
- it offers a range of functionality that it might not be economic to buy
- you do not have to administer the application
- it is claimed it can be cheaper to operate than either in-house or outsourced solutions.

Issues that concern potential users centre around data security. These include compliance with the Data Protection Act, allowing sensitive data to be held by third parties and the threat of hacking. In addition to security worries, there is the problem of inflexibility. You have little room to suit your own needs: pretty much you have to accept the system/ application as given. This may make the approach simpler but leaves little scope to adapt to suit your particular needs.

Forms of insourcing

There will be some organizations that will have conducted a cost–benefit analysis and come to the conclusion that services should not be outsourced. There are other organizations that believe, almost as a matter of principle, that better cost and/or service can be provided in house. They believe that knowledge of the organization and its culture and processes is vital to provide a good service. However you arrived at this view, there are still decisions to be made. Do you set up an internal subsidiary company, at arm's length from the rest of the organization, to provide shared services? Will this 'subsidiary' sell its services externally? Do you instead create a separate profit centre within the mainstream organization, or merely a cost centre? More conventionally, are shared services integrated into the normal work of the HR department? The outcome of your thinking is likely to be affected by whether you intend to:

- sell your services externally
- offer them to other parts of the business, e.g. internationally
- create SLAs with your business partners
- count HR costs as part of a corporate overhead.

Those answering 'yes' at the top of the list are likely at least to create separate cost centres, whilst those treating HR costs as an overhead are unlikely to see the worth of a discrete business within the function. You will also want to align your approach with what is happening elsewhere in the organization – how other support functions manage this matter.

So, as Figure 3.1 shows, a shared services centre may be an integrated service provider. It may then go from being a budget cost centre to a profit centre, expected to generate its own income to cover its costs. This may be the precursor to operational independence as a subsidiary, expected to generate profits in the same way as any other business.

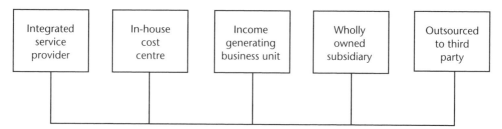

Figure 3.1   Different service provision options

Source: Reilly and Tamkin (1996)

SEPARATE (COMMERCIAL) ENTITY

There are advantages in creating a discrete business that sells services to other group companies. It means it can be properly assessed on a cost–benefit basis. Its relationship with customers needs to be, and is, on a commercial footing. Its business objectives can be focused and targets made clear. Yet this can nearly as easily be done through a profit or cost centre (see below). So why would you go to the trouble of setting up a subsidiary company? The main reasons are:

- If you want to sell services externally and the cost/profit can be ring-fenced.
- You see this as the precursor to outsourcing – getting the service in best shape to be taken over by a contractor. This can be done from an integrated profit centre but is easier from a subsidiary.
- You have a complicated group structure and having a third party organization means you can sell services more easily to each of the independent businesses.

Companies like BT created a discrete business and then moved further along the spectrum shown in Figure 3.1 towards creating a separate joint venture company. Some other organizations with similar capabilities, in size, reach or technology, have given themselves the option of selling services to third parties, but have not yet done so, preferring to give first attention to getting their internal service provision right.

EXAMPLE 3.10

With the growing interest in outsourcing HR activities, BT decided to exploit its scale and technology to sell its services externally. So it established a profit centre based wholly on internal capability. Before long, BT moved towards greater external positioning. Together with Accenture it established a completely discrete joint venture company, expected to run as an independent business. This is called e-PeopleServe. Around 1100 staff transferred into the new company from BT. (IDS, 2000)

INTERNAL COST OR PROFIT CENTRE

The difference between cost and profit centres is that the former is based on simply costing out services based on pure expense budgets, whereas the latter will build in an element of margin on top of cost to meet internal profit or rate of return targets. Thus cost centres aim purely at cost recovery, whereas profit centres strive for income generation.

The advantages of having a separate cost or profit centre are:

- It makes for more commercial relationships. Only those services that are really required are provided. Putting a charge on them makes customers think more carefully as to whether they really want them.
- It encourages good monitoring. You need to know service usage, expenditure and other metrics as you would in any business.
- It allows you to ring-fence the shared service offering from other parts of HR, especially if the latter are not charging out their costs and are compulsory to business users.
- It provides very transparent costs which helps monitoring but also benchmarking. This makes it easier to judge where outsourcing would be appropriate.

Its disadvantages are:

- It can generate excessive and unnecessary bureaucracy. It can be 'excessive' in the same way as with outsourcing (see the points made above) because it requires an extensive monitoring process, and 'unnecessary' because it is 'funny' not real money changing hands. All the transactions stay within the business; money does not pass to contractors.
- Its very separateness of an independent unit can mean that it becomes cut off from the rest of the function. Communication becomes more difficult. Different priorities emerge. It means satisfying the short-term customer needs in the service centre, to be contrasted with looking after the future corporate interests of the business – the emphasis to be expected from the central HR team.

EXAMPLE 3.11

In one financial services company shared services were set up as a profit centre, charging each of the businesses for services provided. This was done at business-head level. Service level agreements were concluded so that volume, cost and quality of service could be reported. Line managers were seen as prime customers, though there was a close relationship with HR managers too. The shared services operation treated itself as an external provider and so had continuously to face the challenge of being externally competitive. The centre put itself in the position of being outsourced should the company wish to do so.

How is it managed?

There is then the question of who manages the shared services operation? If shared services are located within the mainstream organization, then it would be common to put them under the auspices of the corporate headquarters. If it is part of HR, it is usual that they report either directly to the HR director or to one of his/her subordinates. This is shown graphically in Figure 3.2. Figure 3.2 positions the shared services centre as interposed between the corporate organization and the business units. The HR managers facing the business units may report either to HR or the business units.

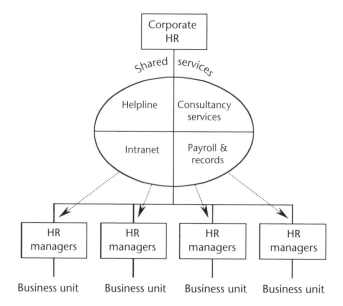

Figure 3.2   Management of the shared services operation

Source: Reilly (1999)

Where the shared services centre is part of a service organization then the reporting lines go the other way round: shared services report to a general service manager/director with a dotted line to HR.

EXAMPLE 3.12

Powergen began with a shared services concept back in 1993. The centre is a £1.5 million business, employing up to 30 people including a payroll service. It provides services to some 40 business units, mostly under annual contract. It is expected to cover its costs by charging out its services. It reports to the Services Division Director, with a dotted line to the HR Director. The latter is a meaningful relationship shown by the fact that the HR Services Manager has a monthly meeting with the HR Director in the chair, divisional HR Managers, corporate HR staff and a selection of HR users. The aim is to sort out boundary issues, co-ordinate activities and tie HR work together.

Where shared services is more separate there is greater variation in the management of the operation. In extreme cases this may be just like the relationship between a subsidiary and its parent company. It might be quite independent with very light overseeing by the parent. Assuming it is a profit centre, then it may be judged on its profitability and nothing more.

EXAMPLE 3.13

Hertfordshire National Health Service's (NHS's) HR shared services operation provides support to nine organizations. The HR director who runs the service reports to a board made up of customers, though she formally reports currently to the local health authority. Their work is monitored against national and local targets. This approach works well, but if there were to be problems, the lack of a single point of accountability may prove difficult.

Cross-organizational provision

INTERNALLY

Which parts of your organization are brought together into the shared service centre is not a self-evident decision. If you are a small or simply constructed organization then the decision may not be difficult. But if you are responsible for a more complex, multidivisional or international company, then which parts of the organization are to be included, and how, is more difficult.

One decision axis concerns geography. Do you have a series of shared services centres for each country; do you do it on a regional basis or even globally? For example, do you aim for a global payroll facility, a global call centre, a global benefits office or one for the UK only? How you combine services does depend upon what you are combining. The greater the diversity of policy and practice the more likely national systems will prevail. It is more difficult to manage employee relations internationally or to manage those issues heavily affected by national employment law. Reward structures may be very different from country to country. It is easier in theory to combine straightforward transactional or information services, but even here there are differences in language and HR practice that have to be accounted for. HR information systems would have to be multilingual for use across many countries, and payroll systems would have to reflect the reward and tax mechanisms that are usually very different from country to country. To operate an international call centre or make use of a global intranet, you either have to require employees to speak and read a common language (and this is the case for some English-speaking multinationals) or use linguists to provide the oral or written service. Even with a common service offering, how call centres are used will vary from country to country for cultural reasons. Naturally, HR administration that relates to expatriates or to company-wide processes (e.g. a share scheme) is easier to support transnationally.

Consultancy services are perhaps the easiest of all activities to combine regionally or even globally. Advice on, say, organization design, training and development or performance management can be provided by advisers who are able to adapt general company principles to the needs within specific environments. Similarly, centres of excellence can develop broad policy frameworks that might offer either a philosophy within which individual operating companies can operate or more detailed policy for a global management cadre. For the latter, succession planning, remuneration and development may be organized on a corporate basis.

Besides practical considerations, the decision on how to organize shared services should be also determined by the reasons for setting up the service function in the first place. Scale brings cost efficiencies, scope brings improved service through better knowledge sharing. For larger organizations scale benefits can be considerable but there is a risk of producing the lowest common denominator in service quality. Yet real cost savings should be realized. Alternatively, giving a bespoke service to each country may offer benefits to customers in the scope of the service on offer, but with a high price tag.

EXAMPLE 3.14

IBM has an HR service based in Portsmouth (AskHR), handling phone calls and emails from nearly 100 000 customers, managers and staff, in a growing number of countries across Europe – up to 17 by 2001, from Italy to Finland. This means that three-quarters of the call centre staff in Portsmouth are not UK nationals. Eleven different languages are used. (IDS, 2001)

Shell People Services employs a team of 700 staff organized regionally to provide services to Shell companies in Europe, the USA, Australia and New Zealand. Services include recruitment, expatriation, HR-IT, payroll, compensation and benefits, HR organization development (OD) and diversity consultancy, learning and job evaluation. Globally they are in the process of implementing a common HR information system based on SAP/R3.

Besides geography, shared services can be structured around business units. Thus production or sales might each have their own centre. These might be nationally organized or have an international dimension.

EXAMPLE 3.15

In its first use of shared services, the BBC had separate centres in different businesses. News, Resources and the Corporate business units all had their own shared services operation. It was subsequently decided to combine them together to achieve economies of scale and emphasize the togetherness of the one organization. Nevertheless, within the common service centre, staff specialize in supporting particular business units.

Those companies with subsidiary operations will have to decide whether they will include them in the corporate shared services or leave them separate, either to have their own shared services centre or work to a different HR model. This question arises particularly after a merger or acquisition. Where the driver has been cost saving, then pulling together activities into a single shared services centre will be attractive. Where the intention is to leave the acquisition with a distinctive market position then HR integration may be less desirable.

EXAMPLE 3.16

The Prudential started shared services some nine years ago. Gradually, different businesses have been added to the main business. Successively, M&G, Egg and Scottish Amicable have been served from a common centre.

EXTERNALLY

Besides outsourcing, cross-organization collaboration is another form of externally combined service. This involves separate organizations coming together to share facilities. It is easier to conceive of this idea if you are in the public sector. This is because ultimately the public, through central or local government or some other agency, is the 'owner' of the activity. Outwith a competitive environment, sharing might be thought also to bring the benefits of economies of scale, reducing cost and building expertise. It is also an attractive alternative to the politically more fraught outsourcing to a third party. Even in the private sector, if your organization can ally itself with others with similar needs, there are savings to be made in sharing development and operating costs. For these reasons it may become more common. Some financial services companies have already contemplated linking with non-competing companies with which they already have a business relationship. Some privatized utilities are exploring whether to share the administration of pensions arrangements that pre-date privatization. Local authorities have considered banding together to obtain economies of scale in HR administration. A particular service might be hosted by one authority on behalf of the others or outsourced to a third party provider. The NHS already has examples where trusts have combined their HR services as a cost-saving measure. For example, six Lothian-based NHS trusts combined their HR services for this reason (Industrial Relations Services, 1998).

EXAMPLE 3.17

In the NHS in Hertfordshire there is a central HR service provided to the local health authority, Hertfordshire Partnership Trust (an amalgam of previously discrete services including mental health, learning disability and children's services) and Primary Care Trusts plus the new Strategic Health Authority.

To these discrete organizations it offers a wide ranging service:

- centralized recruitment
- employee relations
- advice on HR strategy
- managing change
- organization development or design
- workforce planning
- facilitation of training and development
- HR administration.

To the local acute hospitals (that are also wholly separate entities within the NHS, but much larger and physically concentrated) the HR shared service offers a different service. It is working in partnership on issues such as training and development and co-ordinated recruitment approaches. This may be progressively extended, but is unlikely to include employee relations, strategic or change management support.

Each organizational component within the core group currently has a 'lead consultant' who tackles the business specific issues, but he or she is part of the central team, not an employee of the organization they support.

Devolvement

Your introduction of shared services might be accompanied by the desire to devolve a range of people activities to line managers to undertake in place of HR. This has been a general trend for some time. It has been primarily motivated by a desire to increase local account-ability, but also to speed decision-making and reduce the size of the HR function. Moreover, it has been seen as a vital element in the repositioning of HR, getting way from its 'nanny' role and from low-level tasks to higher value-added activities. As such, launching shared services is an ideal opportunity to reconsider the relationship between HR and the line.

EXAMPLE 3.18

Phil Dick of Royal & SunAlliance reported at the IIR Shared HR Services Conference (Dick, 2000) that a key objective of their HR review was for 'line managers to take responsibility for the management, training and development of their teams, and for HR to provide improved management information to assist this'.

The Prudential aims for 'self-sufficiency' among its managers.

In practice, what is devolved varies greatly. Do you devolve activities (doing things) or responsibilities (being accountable for things)? Do you take the same approach for each topic – do you treat reward the same as training? In general, it is likely that policy direction and process design remain with HR, but many practical people management tasks would switch (if they were not already there) to line management. Common activities of this sort include:

- job design and work organization
- selection and recruitment
- employee relations
- performance management
- routine administration (e.g. recording holidays or sickness)
- direct people management (e.g. discipline or welfare).

On some of these subjects there can helpfully be a line–HR partnership at work. Thus recruitment interviewing may be done together; in more serious discipline or performance management cases HR gets involved. New technology is in fact pushing out the boundaries of what line managers do. Organizations are making use of on-line facilities that enable managers to change people's salaries. HR may set the rules of the game, but allow managers to make the decisions. This keeps HR out of the day-to-day issues, both in terms of operationalizing their policies and in their administration – these salary updates bypass HR being entered from the manager's desk straight to payroll.

Deciding what should remain part of HR and what should move to line management will depend upon a number of factors. You should consider:

- What will go with the grain of the organization? In other words, is responsibility passed to line managers on other business activities? Is there a general decentralization of accountability to operating units?
- Are all business units of like mind? Do some want devolvement and greater responsibility for people matters or are they happy for HR to remove this 'burden'. Can you manage such differences in demand?
- What skills do line managers possess? Are they equipped to deal with more people-related activities?

- Do they have the time and resources?
- Do they want more responsibility?
- Are employees confident that managers are equipped to undertake these duties in a fair, consistent and effective manner?
- Do those HR staff who support line managers have the skills to advise, guide and encourage without taking over or abdicating responsibility?

These are important questions to consider before embarking on devolvement, because getting it wrong can cause problems later. Managers may feel overwhelmed by workload, feel overly exposed to take responsibility for matters outwith their skills or staff may doubt managers' capability and miss the independent professionalism of HR staff. At a practical level, managers may set up rival administrative systems or hire support staff to cope with the burden placed upon them. These problems will be described in more detail in Chapter 9.

There are implications, too, for the management of shared services. At a simple level, if HR does not perform a task it is not a candidate for a shared services centre. But the issues are more significant than that. If line management does have extensive people activities under its care, then it is more likely that the shared services function will be interacting significantly with them as customers. This might be in receiving data to process (from absence statistics to pay increases) or receiving calls on the interpretation of policy (e.g. on disciplinary or poor performance cases). Much of the former role will disappear the more that managers can input their own data. So devolvement and self-service are linked items, and it is the latter to which we now turn.

Self-service and web-based services

Employee self-service or the broader concept of e-HR refers to the electronic means by which staff can gain information, add data to systems, carry out transactions or, even, do modelling. In the most developed approaches (typically found in IT companies) the result is a fully integrated, organization-wide electronic network of HR-related data, information services, databases, tools and applications, that are generally accessible at any time by employees, managers and HR professionals. Corporate intranets are the means by which this is done initially. These are becoming increasingly common, as the technology gets cheaper and easier to use. Thereafter, direct access to employee records systems or even payroll are the follow on steps.

Most forms of HR intranet start by providing information. Employees can look up company policy on, say, compassionate leave, travel allowances or learning subsidies. Managers (and employees, too, if they so wish) can look at disciplinary policies, policies on reward or performance management.

This can go further by managers or employees downloading forms for completion and onward transmission, electronically or not. Managers might download a job evaluation questionnaire, the format of a job description or the performance appraisal document. Employees could use interactive mechanisms to book a training course or apply for a job on the internal job advertising system.

Introducing intranets can be the precursor to giving wider access to employee data and, in some instances, allowing its manipulation. Already line managers are being given on-line access to employee records, as yet with limited update rights. This is likely to be the stepping stone to managers authorizing changes to pay or loading details on new recruits, authorized and actioned directly. Access to personal data might be extended to employees to allow them to alter their personal records. This may start with purely factual, relatively static data (e.g. marital status), but could become more sophisticated in relation to dynamic information, e.g. by encouraging employees to maintain training records, develop a skills inventory, express career development aspirations, compile a curriculum vitae and so on.

More sophisticated computing power may be devoted to modelling systems. An obvious example is in flexible benefits. Individuals are able to model the impact of the choices available to them, say trading pay against holidays or extra pension provision against a bigger car. Mass customization of terms and conditions is possible, as all variations and combinations can be recorded and monitored on the computer.

Decision support mechanisms are another development. These can allow managers to make better decisions on such things as discipline, training or selection. Managers are electronically taken down a decision tree that enables them to see what options are initially available, but it leads them to make the right choice in their circumstances. So a manager faced with an employee with a weakness in customer service may be probed by the computer on the specific problem area and then have a specific remedy proposed, be it a training course or coaching mechanism.

Proactive pull technology gets employees or managers to think about the implications of, for example, changes in their personal circumstances. So if an employee notifies the system that they have got married, a prompt is generated asking if the beneficiary of death service provision should be adjusted. Administrators use this technology to good effect. It may help manage a maternity case efficiently by not only reminding the user of when actions need to be taken, but that certain situations should lead to other actions (e.g. a woman resigning during her maternity leave would prompt the administrator to set in train a number of actions).

So self-service can move from a passive state (where users can read on-line information) through basic electronic transactions to more complex interactions. Intranet information may be the start. Customized email, allowing material to be automatically sent and received within the organization or through external links, may be the next step. On-line meetings and project collaboration may be permitted as a way of creating more of a virtual workplace to sit alongside (or, in fewer cases, replace) the physical work environment.

EXAMPLE 3.19

At BP employees can access myHR.net, a self-service web portal. This allows them to update their own personal record, to revise their benefits package, to book training courses, to calculate relocation assistance or an expatriate package, to post their skills and career interests, and to apply for a transfer via the job vacancy system. (IDS, 2000)

Ease of access to computers will be an important determinant of how far and fast e-HR is launched. In some organizations, nearly all employees have a desktop computer. Those that do not would be able through computer kiosks to get on line. Kiosks or similar facilities naturally work best with a physically concentrated and stable workforce. It is more difficult to provide access to peripatetic workers who may rarely set foot in conventional offices. However, mobile communication equipment (e.g. via mobile phones) is likely to solve even this problem – albeit with a cost attached.

Speed of progress within an organization will probably not be determined by technological capability alone, but also by the culture – how much is the organization prepared to devolve responsibility to line managers or employees? This poses the more fundamental question about what role the HR function should have in a self-service environment, as discussed in Chapter 9. Some managers in organizations do still expect the HR function to deal with job vacancies, to undertake disciplinary cases, to improve absence rates through hands-on illness management, and so on. Whatever the HR function may wish to achieve in being more strategic and extricating itself from such operational activities, in part through introducing a self-service facility, the function has to be mindful of its customer demands. This makes the role of HR and its relationships with customers a key question to answer when contemplating a move to self service.

Why consider e-HR options? The following benefits are to be found:

- cost savings through needing fewer people in HR to deal with queries or transactions as they are managed on line
- better quality information on the system as those with the knowledge or expertise have loaded the material
- improved management information based on better records
- higher levels of knowledge sharing and collaborative working across organizational boundaries
- better productivity, if management time is no longer diverted to HR administration
- far greater proportions of the workforce able to work remotely, at any time for more of the time
- more sophisticated and informed decision-making
- empowerment of staff so that they have more control over their lives and providing them with easier access to information.

EXAMPLE 3.20

Cisco, the Internet equipment company, claims to have saved £36 million by automating HR administration, including applying employee self-service, and achieved similar levels of savings. Induction and related training using web-based tools have proved popular with managers, as have on-line pay reviews. Routine tasks, like handling expenses, are done automatically unless a manager lodges an objection. Links are being established to service providers, such as health care, to allow employees to contact them directly. (Trapp, 2001)

But there are disadvantages with e-HR. Introducing e-HR is not cheap, especially if you do not have the computer infrastructure in place, be it in the physical kit or software design. Some features may have a quick payback period (on-line pay slips or e-recruitment), whereas others may take longer to justify themselves and in ways that are not so quantifiable (e.g. e-learning). Implementation may be slow and time-consuming. The Hunter Group Inc. (2000) reports that it may take a year to implement a single e-facility. For e-HR to be a success you have to have a system that meets people's needs in terms of speed, stability and easy navigation. You have to ensure that security concerns are properly taken care of, so that the chances of internal fraud and external hacking can be mitigated. You may be right that HR staff numbers can be cut, but IT support will increase. Overemphasis on computer-based interaction can lead to some dysfunctional effects. Those with easy access to computers or who are familiar with them in their work may quickly make use of e-HR, but those whose access is not so straightforward may feel disadvantaged. Ensuring all your staff are computer literate may be another significant investment cost. People stop talking to each other but communicate electronically. Some of the subtleties of face-to-face interaction are lost, leading to a greater risk of misunderstandings. Remote and impersonal contact can deal with simple and straightforward issues, but not with the more complex ones. This may mislead people into thinking that problems are easier than they are. There is also the impact of 'technological creep' to consider, This refers to the '24 × 7' working model that means that employees cannot escape work and this poses serious questions for their balance between home and office life. Technology can become an end in itself rather than a means to another end. Staff can be left spending a disproportionate amount of time on an organizational intranet. There is evidence from the USA that playing with flexible benefit plans can distract people from their work and be a significant source of inefficiency.

You have to take into account the impact on HR – its change of role – and its capability to deal with this new, more electronic, world. Staff will have to become comfortable with handling information and queries in a different way. Some may not rise to this challenge. Similarly, if third party providers are in some way involved, these will have to be successfully managed. Do your HR colleagues have the skills to do this? These thoughts should be borne in mind when we look later at HR capability in step 5 of the process of introducing shared services.

EXAMPLE 3.21

In 2000 the project Director for Marks and Spencer (M&S) people solutions programme told a PeopleSoft conference that 'Fifty-five per cent of M&S employees have never used a PC, and most store employees do not have a desk'. To overcome these problems Marks and Spencer is installing computer booths and training staff to use the technology. 'Self service is hard work' (Deeks, 2000, p. 9).

These risks are presented not as reasons to avoid e-HR but arguments for you to take care in how it is launched and how it is used. If it is positioned as a means of more effective management that gives managers and individuals more responsibility for relevant personnel data, you should have more success than if it is perceived to be glossy gimmick or toy. It may be that the technology has to be phased in either to ease the investment cost or to recognize the varied IT skills profile of your workforce. But in the end you need to create a new culture of people doing things for themselves if e-HR is to work.

Location of services

Another area of debate concerns how the shared services are physically delivered. One view is that technology enables the service to be executed by people who are widely dispersed, even when completing the same function. Thus, for example, payroll entries could be made at a number of different sites. This is then a *virtual* shared service centre, with a common management structure but distributed execution, and is an argument for a number of centres carrying out similar work within a common organizational and process framework. This may also be politically attractive in that many sites can share the work; you do not have to decide which gets the single centre – thereby offending all the others. Such sensitivity may be greater in a transnational setting. It also allows both common and bespoke work processing, distinguishing that which has to be done in a corporate way from activities that should reflect their national/local needs.

EXAMPLE 3.22

The European HR director of Hewlett Packard, Didier Hirsch, argued that a virtual network is the preferable option. He said of setting up their shared services centre: 'We changed the country based system, but allowed our managers to stay in the same offices. We send the work to the people, not the people to the work' (Rosenbaum, 1999, p. 20).

The alternative position is that, whilst technologically possible to deliver services from a number of physical centres, this defeats a large part of the logic of having shared services. Pulling them together gives the opportunity for optimum resourcing that is more difficult to achieve without co-location. It allows greater economy of scale. Also, co-location helps develop an *esprit de corps* that should generate common and improved service standards. Having staff all in one place allows such techniques as *buddying*, which helps with cover and coaching. Improved learning can also be achieved.

This argument applies both within a type of service – helpline, administrative processing or project support – and across the range of services. There are benefits to the co-location of a combination of different services in the same place:

- Cross-group learning and information flow is better.
- Escalating problems to a higher level of expertise is easier.
- Boundary management of problems is less common.
- For developmental or operational reasons, people can be transferred without difficulty to other work areas.

EXAMPLE 3.23

BOC used the fact that staff were located together to get subject specialists to spend a period of time each month on the helpline to get a better understanding of what pressures their colleagues were under. This helped them when calls were referred to them for specialist advice.

An added argument in favour of co-location comes if the shared service team moves into new office space. This can help both practically (in having custom-designed facilities perhaps with employee input) and psychologically (demonstrating change and creating improved work relationships). Indeed, there is an argument that, whenever possible, new accommodation is found for the introduction of the shared services to demonstrate a break with the past and create a new beginning. This is especially true where existing provision is being brought together under one management stream.

Where should the shared service centre be located? If cost is the predominant reason for sharing services then the lowest, reasonable cost location should be chosen. This will take account of accommodation – an area with relatively low rent or an existing spare building – and labour market rates – an area where recruitment at a reasonable price and high retention should be possible. Where other considerations prevail you might like to site the service centre where:

- you already employ staff doing this or similar kind of work
- you wish to give easy physical access to employees or managers
- there are existing skills in the local labour market.

EXAMPLE 3.24

One large UK organization began with a shared services centre based in London to cover south-east England. This was where the bulk of both HR staff and customers were. Their responsibility was then widened to cover the rest of the UK as administrative work transferred to London from regional offices. Administrative staff in the regions did not transfer as well. Surplus staff were made redundant.

The existing personnel administration activity was combined with payroll in a subsequent move, and the shared services centre relocated from London to Manchester. This took advantage of spare and cheaper office space. Again no staff transferred with the work; new people were hired in Manchester.

When the shared services centre was set up at Guinness some four years ago it looked after the Park Royal brewery and a small site in Runcorn. The centre was centrally placed in the main office block on a relatively small site. This allowed contact between HR staff and employees, who were free to wander in and out of the office. This fitted in with the personal service the HR staff liked to give and was welcomed by the many long-serving employees who were used to dealing face to face. This also applied to new staff who were also familiar with the HR office, as they received their induction there.

At Telewest (IDS, 2001) a number of sites were identified as possible locations for the shared service centre. A greenfield site would be too expensive, likely to be overly remote from current operations and take too long to establish. A Birmingham site was eventually chosen because:

- it already had a number of HR staff already in place
- there was good IT support present
- it was accessible from other sites
- it enjoyed a good local labour market.

Standard Chartered Bank decided to site its shared service centre in Chennai, India. This location was chosen because of the technological infrastructure, skilled workforce and low costs. Having a single centre to support 32 000 employees worldwide made more sense when no one office has more than 5000 employees (Arkin, 2002).

Setting the numbers

Having decided whether to outsource or insource, what will continue to be done by HR or devolved to the line, whether to introduce self-service and where to locate shared services, there is then the question of staffing levels. There are various ways in which the numbers you need can be calculated. Which of the following will be chosen will depend upon the availability/accuracy of the relevant data and what suits your circumstances best.

FINANCIALLY DERIVED

A simple top-down approach is to calculate what numbers can be afforded in the economics of an activity. More specifically, if there is a total sum allocated for staffing costs from the budget, the average cost per head could be determined and the numbers derived.

- *Advantages*: simple to operate; aligns with the budget.
- *Disadvantages*: tells you nothing of who needs to be employed (skills etc.) and does not relate to the changing requirements of the activity.
- *Applicability*: can be used for any workforce group.

RATIOS

These can allow you to determine staffing against another criterion, hopefully some robust business measure. It suits those circumstances where there are clear business outcomes, e.g. number of recruits. The relationship between the two is analysed which should allow you to fix your numbers against expected business performance. It is also frequently used to calculate the need for indirect labour through applying a ratio against total staff. So this might be HR staff number or cost against total workforce number or payroll cost.

- *Advantages*: allows you to fix your numbers against expected business performance. Good in stable circumstances. Allows benchmarking.
- *Disadvantages*: needs initial time spent on analysis and, unless frequently reviewed, assumes an unchanging relationship between the two parts of the equation which does not allow for change (e.g. through lowering costs or increasing output).
- *Applicability*: works better where there is a clear connection between an activity and an outcome. It is also used for support activities, but probably because there is felt to be no better (or cheaper) method.

PROFESSIONAL JUDGEMENT

This can mean exactly what it says or it can be a guesstimate.

- *Advantages*: quick and easy; better in stable circumstances.
- *Disadvantages*: managers are likely to overestimate what is needed (to maximize their resources or because of an underestimation of productivity possibilities). Assumptions are not explicit, which makes responding to subsequent change more difficult.
- *Applicability*: can be used in any circumstances but is particularly dangerous where large numbers of employees are involved and where there is significant change likely.

WORK STUDY

This technique allows you to determine optimal resourcing for a new operation, based on models of ideal productivity. It is based on detailed calculation of such things as the 'standard time' taken to carry out an operation.

- *Advantages*: allows you to determine optimal resourcing. Can take into account the effect of technological or business change.
- *Disadvantages*: intensive effort to do calculations and needs to be kept up to date to be useful. Works well when carried out thoroughly, but can produce poor results if insufficient effort is expended.
- *Applicability*: particularly useful for a new activity to understand resource implications. Much used in the manufacturing, banking and retail sectors where standard tasks are common for large numbers of employees. Where such economies of scale do not apply, it can be too expensive to do properly.

ACTIVITY ANALYSIS

This involves obtaining detailed knowledge of activities using diaries, questionnaires, interviews, etc. It can be used both to look at skills/numbers and to identify areas for improvement in some detail. Thus it can look at present arrangements and suggest how many employees you need for each task, and recommend changes in working practices, in allocation of duties, and in the size and shape of resourcing.

- *Advantages*: gives a thorough understanding of current arrangements and allows changes in numbers, working practices, duties and nature of resources to be recognized. Therefore it provides quality information at the start of a resourcing project.
- *Disadvantages*: time-consuming to do (often outside help is required) and needs to be reviewed periodically to identify changes.
- *Applicability*: this is a good approach to use for administrative staff where work study finds it hard to deal with the variety of the tasks.

TREND DATA

Key relationships can be examined over time. Future forecasts can be based on extrapolating from past data to predict future trends, e.g. to show up productivity improvements.

- *Advantages*: allows key relationships to be examined over time based on hard data showing previous rates of productivity improvement. Best in unchanging activities.
- *Disadvantages*: does not take account of radical change or tell you much about resource needs.
- *Applicability*: most suitable for reasonably predictable activities where change is slow to impact and where forecasts can be helpful.

BUSINESS PROCESS RE-ENGINEERING

This aims to provide a more systematic identification of the means to improve how things are done and linked together that cross current organizational boundaries.

- *Advantages*: is a complete examination of processes, which allows change to be understood.
- *Disadvantages*: was not designed for resource planning, so that it does not necessarily tell you how many staff you need. Requires skilled intervention and co-operative effort to complete.

- *Applicability*: particularly useful as a concept to review those activities which span the organization. May have to be used in combination with another method to be able to calculate the numbers.

BENCHMARKING

You could use the staffing of your sister plant as a guide and, if possible, compare against other similar sites owned by competitors' operations to identify *best practice*. Benchmarking can lead to step changes in what is thought possible, or it may reinforce bad practice – it depends on the performance of the comparators chosen. Care also needs to be taken over making sure like-for-like comparisons are made.

- *Advantages*: gives an external measure of manning and can lead to step changes in what is thought possible. Once a network of contacts is established, this can be used to monitor changes in the external environment.
- *Disadvantages*: can tend to reinforce bad practice, as promote good. Care needs to be exercised to make sure like for like comparisons are made.
- *Applicability*: can be used for all workforce groups, though clearly better for generic activities, e.g. support staff, than for any specialist work.

EXAMPLE 3.25

An energy company used benchmarking to inform their decisions on workforce numbers. It looked at the ratio of HR staff to total staff in a basket of companies. It discovered that the average position was 1:100, excluding training and development and recruitment. It looked, too, at the cost of HR staff as a percentage of operating costs. It also compared its position with its competitors. The conclusion was that their HR staffing was too generous. It gave them a target to aim for in setting their HR resource. Over the next two years the company steadily reduced its numbers to the point where it had reached its 'stretch target' in line with the best in its sector.

Thus each method has its pluses and minuses and the choice should reflect what activities you are looking at as part of the review and the extent to which you want to change them. Business process re-engineering (BPR), for example, gives an insight into work flow and processes. It can challenge the way you organize activities. Work study and activity analysis takes the current task distribution and looks at it in detail. These three techniques build from the bottom through gaining greater understanding of what HR people do and how they relate to each other and their customers. It can be painstaking work but yields deep insights into HR activities. On an evidence basis, it can reject current activities or relocate them. It can stop HR being a 'post office' for certain tasks. It can help decide that recruitment administration should be placed close to recruitment staff or integrated with other administrative activities.

Benchmarking, by contrast, gives a broad-brush overview of your organization's numbers. Some organizations seem to be bewitched by benchmarking, often to obtain simple ratios of HR staff to the workforce population. They believe that by seeing what others do, they get a profound insight into what they should do. If there is a genuine like-for-like comparison, then this may be possible. Unfortunately, it rarely is the case. What is included in HR varies from organization to organization. Even if the HR units can be shaped to make a fair comparison, the business needs are unlikely to be the same. Benchmarking has its place in testing numbers and examining processes in the light of others' experience. Reductionist use of ratios to determine your staffing levels seems misconceived. It does not give sufficient attention to the quality of the service or the needs of the customers and, thus, should only be used as one indicator.

Another source of external data is from HR outsourcing providers. The more sophisticated are developing improved, more robust measures to judge HR numbers. They cost the amount of administration per employee. Currently (2001), the outsourcers' norm is an 'administrative fee' of £400 per employee. As with ratios of HR staff to total workforce, the dangers of like-for-like comparison still remain. But if taken as a broad indication, if your 'administrative fee' is nearer £1000 per employee (as it apparently is with many organizations according to benchmarking organizations such as EP-First (Saratoga), the need for and scale of change is indicated.

Some organizations use internal benchmarking to complement external. They look at simple ratios of another support function's (often finance) staff numbers to the total workforce. Of interest, too, during a general cost reduction exercise is what other functions are doing, what cuts they are making. Having seen what is happening elsewhere, some HR directors will create their own target figure. This is not based on anything more than a 'gut feel' for what level of change the function can stand or what level of numbers reduction is necessary to get the HR team to do things differently. Whilst BPR activity analysis or work study give you detailed information on how your services are configured and allow you to make precise alterations, bold target reductions work on the principle that change will have to come in order to meet the target.

EXAMPLE 3.26

Many organizations have benchmarked their HR numbers, using the ratio of HR staff to total staff. Companies like EP-First (Saratoga) aim to provide comparable data. Many seem to be aiming for a ratio of 1 HR staff member to 100, often moving from a position closer to 1:50.

So our advice would be to use benchmarking, ratios and gut feelings to get a sense of what has to be done to get your HR function in shape. Then use techniques such as activity analysis, work study and/or BPR to get a better appreciation of where changes will need to be made.

Issues in role design

In designing the roles to be performed in the shared service centre, there is a key choice between creating generalist or specialist posts or, more likely, in striking the balance between the two. Most organizations we are familiar with have decided to create generalists in the administrative part of their shared service centre, but with some specialist support. In other words, within their area of responsibility administrative HR staff cover a range of activities (e.g. recruitment administration, payroll changes, maternity absence) as generalists, but with expertise provided (say, in pensions administration) in specific areas. A minority of organizations prefer specialization. This means that all staff handle a specific area of administrative work. They can develop ideas on service improvement, e.g. how to process application forms or sharesave applications. An alternative approach is to allow administrative staff to concentrate on a specific business area, but this may lose some of the resourcing benefits that come from bringing the activities together.

EXAMPLE 3.27

A financial services company has a team of six plus a team leader in its shared services centre. They are organized horizontally by business area as generalists. However, some activities are deemed to be 'team functions', as there is no specialist knowledge required and it evens out workloads. (For example, putting new starters onto the payroll is a team function.) Each individual has a back-up business area to cover. They have people with particular HR expertise in certain areas, sometimes because there has been part of a working group on the subject. But their manager does not like to emphasize experts too much because you can become too reliant on them. After all, they can leave or be away on holiday and this is difficult if others become dependent upon them. Having said that, experts can help or train others, thereby improving knowledge sharing and reducing dependency.

With consultancy or project posts, there is a similar choice to be made. Organizations again tend to opt for generalists capable of handling a wide variety of work, but once more recognizing that there are areas of specialism that need to be performed by experts. However, there is the alternative view that creating specialists allows a concentration of expertise to tackle issues in depth, rather than superficially in the way that may have happened in traditional structures.

One method of balancing the generalism–specialism tension is to ask employees to be all-rounders, but expect them, in addition, to develop an expertise in one subject. Thus project consultants might be capable of tackling any issue, but each might specialize in handling a particular case, be it to do with resourcing or training. Similarly, administrative assistants might do all kinds of work, but develop a deeper knowledge on, say, managing share option benefits.

The approach adopted depends in part on whether there are centres of excellence, where they are located and how they are staffed. If they form part of the shared services centre and are resourced by genuine experts, then a generalist approach to consultancy is more likely to be successful.

Table 3.1 illustrates what the distinction between generalism and specialization might look like in practice.

The benefits and disbenefits of creating generalists and specialists should be obvious. Having the former gives more resource flexibility in being able to balance work demands with the staff available. In individual development terms, employees can grow a wide knowledge of subject areas. Its disadvantage is that people become jacks of all trades and masters of none. Specialization, by comparison, avoids the problem of spreading knowledge too thinly, but risks staff complaints that work is too repetitive. The latter is a persuasive argument: some work, especially administrative, needs variety to make it palatable. This means that some tasks may have to be done on a rotational basis, e.g. telephone helplines, to avoid overstressing staff. Other areas of work are too complex, e.g. managing pensions administration, to be done by anyone other than someone specifically trained. The hope is that the work is rich enough to prevent boredom. The danger of rotating this sort of work is that you underestimate the depth of professional expertise, even in administrative activities, and inexperience leads to mistakes.

Table 3.1 Generalist or specialist roles in shared service centres

Area of activity	Generalist role	Specialist role
Administrative services	All forms of record/payroll changes	Distinction between those who handle payroll changes from other records
	Management of all forms of cases, e.g. sickness, maternity	Experts in maternity, sickness absence, etc.
	Administration of various benefit schemes, e.g. health insurance	Specialist in car fleet management, recruitment support, etc.
Consultancy/project support	Tackles any form of project for any client	Alignment with specific businesses covering their problems only or Work on issues only within specific subject area (e.g. reward or development)
Helplines or other means of information or advice	Rotation of staff between activities, i.e. manning the help desk one day, then doing detailed casework the next and working on improving information on the intranet on the day following	Concentration on particular methods of support. So working exclusively on the phone, doing intensive casework or improving published procedures

Source: Reilly (1999)

EXAMPLE 3.28

Compaq splits its shared service centre staff into two pairs. One pair looks after joiners and leavers; the other pair processes changes to terms and conditions and management information. Every six months they swop roles. (IDS, 2001)

At JP Morgan they aim for staff to stay only for nine to 12 months in their 'client centre'. 'It was definitely a fear that people thought they would get stuck in the call centre' said Rita Carrig, the centre's manager (Pickard, 2000, 34).

Transco's service centre staff are encouraged to do Chartered Institute of Personnel Development (CIPD) qualifications and to work in other HR areas on secondment, and later transfer. (Pickard, 2000)

Another aspect of role design is how you connect together your various tasks, especially those that are customer facing with those that are engaged in policy design. One common solution is to use escalation procedures. This means that if, for example, a call comes in to the helpline asking for information, it can be dealt with by the service operator, but if the caller then starts asking for interpretation of policy, then the operator is required to pass the caller to a higher level of support. This may be so complicated a question that it goes to a policy specialist, or it may be dealt with at the next rung up the ladder. The problem may require a more intensive follow-up, so that it gets treated as a 'case'. The example below illustrates an escalation procedure.

EXAMPLE 3.29

One organization has the following service levels:

1 Information management.
2 Case management.
3 Advisory service.
4 Specialist support.

At level 1, informants are given basic information, say, about terms and conditions of employment or company procedures. Cases are referred to level 2 if they require more time or a degree of interpretation. If they are more complicated still, because of policy complexity or the unique circumstances, then an advisory service is used. Finally, specialist expertise in, say, reward or resourcing tackles issues that are more to do with policy changes.

Conclusion

In this chapter we have looked at the big design decisions you have to confront. As a reminder, the key questions are:

- Do you carry out all the shared services activities yourself or do you outsource all/some for third parties to do on your behalf?
- If you outsource, what sort of contractual arrangement do you seek – transactional, partnership or co-sourced?
- If you retain the shared services work, how do you structure the activity – integrated into the rest of the company or separated as a subsidiary?
- Do you want your shared services to make a profit, either from selling its wares internally or externally?
- Do you link together with any other organization to share costs and expertise?
- To what extent are you going to devolve people activities, previously done by HR, to line managers to do? This will impact on the nature of the work of your shared services centre.
- What part will technology play in your shared services set-up? Will it be limited to using a corporate intranet or will employees and/or their managers self-serve?
- Will you co-locate your shared services activities or disperse them geographically or in line with your organizational structure?
- How will you go about setting the numbers to be employed in your HR operation? Which methodology will you use?

- What approach will you take to designing the roles in your operation? Will you aim for maximum flexibility and aim for all-rounders, will you prefer to create specialist position or will you opt for a mixture of the two, depending upon the post?

Having asked yourself these questions, we turn to the important process issues that you need to consider before you can implement a new HR model.

4 How to introduce shared services: the process steps to take

However good your design, you will not succeed if your process from getting from where you are now to where you want to be is inadequate. It is often the process aspects of change that get neglected. As one NHS manager said, reflecting upon the setting up of shared services: 'If we did this all over again we would appoint a project manager, make sure there is capacity to make it work, ensure clear leadership, involve stakeholders at an early stage, be clear in our purpose and proposals, and avoid changing at busy times of the year' (Keep, 2001). These are the type of points that get neglected in rushing from the idea to the execution. It may be that you do not have, or are not given much time, to reform your HR department, but even within time constraints you should observe the key principles that underpin this chapter:

- Make sure your senior managers are supportive.
- Get the resources to run a proper project and observe project discipline.
- Establish the quality of your current service – find out its faults.
- Know your own HR staff – what is their current standard and what are they capable of?
- Assess your technology – what needs to be done to improve it?
- Test your design ideas with your HR colleagues and customers, and formally consult with employee representatives at the appropriate moment.
- Get senior management backing for your firm proposals.
- Design your jobs in detail.

Step 1: Commitment to change

The first place to start in any change process is to secure the support of your senior management. If senior managers do not support change then, however much you believe you can argue for it, it will not happen. Indeed it may be that it is the executive committee that is pressing for things to alter. But it would be better if it is you in the HR function that is the vanguard of change, not taking up the rear. You can then steer the direction and define the methodology. The alternative is that the executive defines the problem and decides the solution. Moreover, instead of sending the signal that HR is a strategic change agent, doing the bidding of others reinforces the impression that your function is reactive and directionless.

It is a matter of tactics how the senior management is brought on board. It also depends upon how self-evident are the issues, be they problems to be resolved or benefits to be seized, and how obvious is the approach to be taken. If the issues are not clear, you may have to gather evidence, as in Step 3, before the executive is prepared to commit itself. More commonly, if HR says it needs to alter its service provision and sets out a sensible methodology of how it intends to redesign its processes, most executive committees would endorse HR's action, subject, no doubt, to agreeing the final structure and cost.

At this stage you must define the project's objectives and success criteria, as so many decisions and actions are determined by why the shared services function is being established. This may mean, as Chapter 2 indicated, that the organization may primarily be interested in saving money, improving quality and meeting customer needs, or a combination of the three. Change may be initiated as part of a wider organizational review, it may be enabled by technology or lead to the repositioning of the HR function – but these may be subsidiary reasons as far as senior management is concerned. In the final analysis, the executive might want to see a cheaper service with costs taken out of the HR function, be they of headcount, accommodation or purchased services. Or it may want to see a higher quality service, better meeting customer requirements. This could mean more effective transactional services, but it could mean a greater 'transformational' contribution at the strategic level. You may need to make clear to senior management the risk of not changing. This might emphasize that your HRIS needs upgrading and this is the opportunity to move to employee self-service linked to an HR shared services approach. You might point out that management has been seeking better and more consistent information on employee trends across the company that is impossible to achieve without sharing a common administrative system. Poor information may result in poor resourcing decisions. Then there is competitive argument to deploy. By sticking with the current way of managing HR, you are falling behind your competitors in terms of cost and quality of service delivery. Whatever the particular arguments, it is worth remembering that senior executives may be convinced by positive and/or negative reasons.

It is better to set the question of the HR service in a wider context. If not, your senior management team may view this issue as merely a question of getting a more effective and efficient delivery. It then becomes a technical design problem. Setting the debate into the wider context means establishing a vision of what HR, and people management more generally, should look like in the future. This will involve consideration of:

- What degree of freedom should be permitted to business units in the way they manage people and in the HR policies and practices? In other words, will we operate a centralized model to emphasize efficiency, consistency and commonality, leaving business units with little freedom for innovation? Or is the approach to be one of decentralization – business units are free to pursue their own HR philosophy, but may make use of common services where they wish to. Is a compromise model possible? The centre sets a framework within which business units operate, with certain policies, practices and processes mandated for reasons of either efficiency or corporacy.
- What is the right balance to be found in the HR role between strategic contribution, operational support and administrative service? This means surfacing explicitly the type of role HR should play both in the corporate centre and in the business units.
- The relationship between HR and line management – how much HR work should be devolved? This may be more of a statement of principle at this stage, and relates to the above question. Philosophically, does the organization take the view that managers manage their people and HR is merely there to give them professional advice as required? Or is the approach that HR should relieve managers as much as possible of the administrative burden, leaving them to concentrate on the job they are paid to do?
- How much activity should be automated out through an e-HR approach? This can help

solve the problem both for managers and for HR of relieving elements of tedium from the work. But it requires significant investment that will only be backed if the broader benefits are obvious.

These principles and objectives need to be made clear at the outset of the project, so that subsequent proposals have to be judged against defined criteria and, if implemented, monitoring can be undertaken again with a specific purpose. If objectives are not agreed, later discussion of proposals will be more difficult because senior managers will be approaching issues from diverse standpoints. Moreover, even if decisions are made, the operation of any new approach to HR is in danger of being criticized from several angles. If the finance director thinks that shared services is a cost saving device, he/she will not be impressed by the argument that the service has improved if the cost of delivery has risen. Similarly, there may be some directors who want a better HR contribution and are prepared to pay for it: cost savings will not cut any ice with them if they perceive that HR is still not adding sufficient value.

You should test out senior management thinking, using the reasons set out in Chapter 2. Get them to prioritize or determine what is most important to the organization. Then have this signed off by the team so as to avoid the potential for perceived failure later. If the executive wants a 20 per cent cost saving, then they should understand the consequences. Reductions of this size means exploiting economies of scale and obtaining efficiency from standardized processes. If this is achieved it should not lead to later criticism about lack of service flexibility. You cannot have low cost and bespoke services. Similarly, if service quality and customer-centric objectives are set, large cost savings are difficult to achieve. It is implicit in meeting customer demands that offering variety is more expensive than providing a single product.

To obtain clarity, you may need to push your top team to make plain their views and build a consensus. It is all too easy for busy (and possibly ill-informed) people to gloss over the issues. They may give the impression of agreeing but not really buy in. This becomes more important at Step 8, when you present firm proposals, but even at this stage you need agreement on your present problem or prized goal.

This thinking may argue for more of a workshop setting to talk these issues through than the traditional presentation and discussion. It probably also suggests some informal sounding out of the members of your top team first, to address specific issues they might have personally or that concern their business or function.

Step 2: Establishing a project team and methodology

Once you have senior management endorsement to proceed, it would be appropriate to set up a project team. It may be that parts of the team are in place already through having to put together the high-level case to senior management to change the approach to HR. It may be necessary later to add to the team as the work grows. But even at this early stage it is worth getting a group together to plan what needs to be done and to execute some tasks. These will include:

- defining project objectives
- setting timescales
- identifying resource needs

- clarifying tasks, e.g.:
  - gathering customer opinion
  - establishing costs of the current HR provision
  - benchmarking against other organizations
  - looking at technological needs
  - establishing risks and contingencies.

All this assumes that the approach you wish to use is an involving one. By that we mean, rather than deciding at the top of the organization what it is you want and driving that down through the organization, you build up views from the bottom. Imposition may be appropriate if costs have to be taken out and you expect resistance. If, however, the aim is to build a true *shared* service model then you need to consult your customers. Failure to do so, is likely to result in a much more problematic start to their new service delivery mode as the aims of your restructuring will be not be understood and the solutions you propose will be challenged.

Another important question at this stage is what level of external help will be required, if any. Some of this help may be necessary to supplement your own resources – to give more 'firepower'. Some external assistance may be useful to give an independent and objective assessment, e.g. in getting the views of customers or looking at the capability of HR staff. For some activities you may need expert advice and guidance, especially with technology or in the design choices. Naturally, if you decide to outsource particular activities then it will be the service provider who will have to tackle a number of these problems, but you will need the usual legal support to handle the outsourcing from your perspective and enough knowledge to establish an appropriate deal.

The sort of external consultants to use depends upon the task to be tackled. If you use them for diagnosis for such things as:

- establishing what the different parts of HR do
- determining the process connections in activities
- establishing customer views of the worth of HR services
- assessing the skills of members of the HR team,

then a broad range of consultants will be available, though specific expertise might be necessary if you undertake process mapping. If you want help with design, e.g.:

- deciding upon how the function should be reconfigured
- the extent of devolvement – the work to be passed to line managers
- the technology to use – call centres, intranets, etc. – and its design
- the roles and numbers of staff to be employed,

then you may need specific organization design and certainly technological capability. Finally, consultants can be used for implementation tasks, e.g.:

- producing new policy and procedure manuals
- training HR staff in their new roles
- communicating your proposals
- promoting the value of a shared service centre.

Some organizations take specialist advice on communication and contract out training or graphic design for communication or promotion materials. It may simply be that with a big change programme under way, extra help may be required for tasks such as writing up policy manuals.

EXAMPLE 4.1

BOC used two types of consultant in their move to shared services. One helped with the design of the service centre. This began with a kind of time and motion study to see how HR spent its time. The other, an IT consultancy, helped get their new HRIS running and ironed out any initial problems.

For your internal team it would be useful to balance HR and line customer involvement and, depending upon the organization, of employee customers too. This team should be capable of:

- establishing customer views
- helping to design the structure
- describing roles
- establishing training requirements.

So they should be able to generate ideas and act as a sounding board. They will not necessarily get involved in some of the more sensitive and personal activities (determining capability and appointing staff) or in formal processes (consultation with employee representatives).

For the project team you need to decide whether the members need to be full time or part time. Are they to be formally seconded from their present activities? The advantage of this is that you can ensure that their 'day job' is looked after in their absence and you can count on proper help – not here today, gone tomorrow.

Once the team is established, you need to determine your project methodology. There are many ways of approaching the task of reviewing the HR function and introducing shared services. Which you use in part relates to the resources available to you, but also to the aim of the changes you wish to make. Crudely, you can use a top-down methodology. Here you would expect to see a very focused project aiming to achieve very specific objectives. This might be suitable for a cost reduction exercise or where management wants to challenge a more traditional view of HR and expects resistance. Alternatively, a 'bottom-up' project methodology may be adopted. This is a high engagement model. It is more likely to be customer focused and to tackle problems from their perspective. It also is more likely to allow the creation of a shared services function to be the catalyst for broader change across the HR function as a whole. It can be used as a change programme dealing with not only structural and service issues, but also the attitudes and behaviours of those in the function.

Step 3: Finding out how good your HR service is

OBTAINING CUSTOMER VIEWS

The views of customers are critical in the justification for change and/or in defining what change is necessary. To begin with you need to be clear on who are HR's customers. This means recognizing that HR has a number of different customers:

- senior management who determine policy direction, and where HR might be expected to make a strategic contribution
- line managers who may be the principal users of HR services
- employees who will also consume services, some the same as line managers, others different
- employee representatives, be they unionized or not
- external bodies. These might be government agencies of one sort or another, suppliers and contractors, etc.

Each of these groups has different needs to satisfy. In establishing these needs, there are various methodologies available:

- a generalized customer service questionnaire that seeks views on various aspects of the service. This can be tailored to the circumstances of the specific group being asked
- a more specific survey to obtain views on particular aspects of the service. Training evaluation forms are an example of this. They are also widely used in recruitment to obtain the opinions of candidates – asking the question, how was it for you?
- discussion groups either of a general or specific nature
- using a customer panel, if one is available. These are often used to track the performance of outsourced work but they can be helpful to evaluate internal services too.

EXAMPLE 4.2

Kent County Council consulted its stakeholders about its Personnel and Development function, and got some very clear messages. Whilst customers were positive about the commitment of individual staff and the importance of the work they do, it was felt that change was essential, especially with respect to:

- clarity of roles
- a more proactive service aligned to the business needs
- greater consistency in standards
- a more flexible response
- improved communication and monitoring.

The next question to ask is which customers are invited to participate in the review and what questions you ask them. At the minimum, you would want to know how they believe the current services are being carried out. Then you would probably want to cover what improvements they would seek. Finally, you might wish to engage them on the shape of a redesigned HR function. It is a matter of tactics and a question of the culture of your organization whether you can ask a completely open-ended question against a blank sheet of paper on what HR should look like, or whether it would be more productive in your environment to put up a 'straw man' proposition in order to get the best feedback. If it is the latter, the timing of this part of the customer viewpoint should be moved to later in the process when the outline proposition is better known. The more radical the intention or the more top down the process, the more likely you are to pose the question when there is a better defined picture of the future design.

You are likely to sound out line managers about the service they receive and would want to receive. This will include the provision of information, advice and support. So what do managers need to know from personnel – policy guidelines, company regulations legal requirements, company principles, etc.? Over what subjects do they need guidance, e.g. the legal aspects of disciplinary cases, recruitment methodologies, options in flexible resourcing, etc.? Support can be in terms of administration and will depend upon the organization's IT capability. In a sophisticated environment with devolved responsibility, managers can directly input payroll changes and employees can change data held on the HRIS. In other circumstances, HR might be giving much more help in terms of processing overtime claims, changes of address, sickness deductions, and so on. Support, though, can also mean giving professional assistance in, say, change management (e.g. over a redundancy exercise) or policy implementation (e.g. over the introduction of a new performance management system). There are also services that line managers might wish to take advantage of in terms of training, recruitment, etc.

Senior managers may well have specific needs to satisfy. These may be more in terms of policy or change management support, in organizational design or strategic direction. But there may be operational help needed for the senior people as a group in terms of reward, resourcing, development or succession planning. The top team may also vary considerably in their views on the role of HR. This may range from those who expect a traditional personnel service of line management support (e.g. on employment law and compensation issues) to those forward-thinking executives who realize that the people resource is its one potential source of genuine competitive advantage that cannot easily be replicated. They want to see the HR function engaged at the strategic level. These different perceptions of the HR function will determine what they expect to see from a review of its role.

Employees, too, will expect a range of things. An important question to ask at an early stage is what help employees should receive from HR. This is a question of how much is delivered to them via their line managers. Some organizations take the view that HR should minimize this help as much as possible. We do not think it desirable to expect managers to be the conduit for all things. They do not have the expertise to answer all the questions that will be posed, nor do they have the time to be a post box for HR. Moreover, a role we believe HR should play is acting as an independent source of information and advice to provide employees with another channel to voice their grievances. So HR may also provide information and advice to employees, and possibly support. The welfare role may have been discontinued in many organizations but some in the public sector still perform it and, in the private sector, counselling or child-care advisers have appeared – albeit this activity is frequently externally provided.

It is likely that you would consult the other stakeholders listed above with respect to specific issues. For example, if some training is carried out as part of a government scheme or carried out in conjunction with the local 'business link' and you are considering changing the interface with the external agency, then you might wish to consult on the advantages/disadvantages of the present situation. Similarly, if some services come from a subcontractor, there may be a need to take their views into account in a review that impacts them. An outsourced payroll provider, for example, will be affected by how payroll changes are notified and by whom. Employee representatives may also have relevant opinions to offer, especially in the employee relations areas where they are involved.

The method used by one consultancy to assess perceptions of quality is illustrated in simplified format in Figure 4.1. It surveys a range of customers to establish what services are important to them and how well the HR function is satisfying them.

	Importance	Effectiveness of service
Senior management		
Operational line		
Employee		
HR		

Figure 4.1   Surveying your customers

Source: Hewitt Associates

Step 4: Establishing the current service quality and cost of HR services

It is very easy in reviews of this kind to run away in search of solutions before establishing the problem. Customers have views on the services HR currently provides, but these are perceptions of reality. It is a good idea to gather data to substantiate these perceptions or to challenge them. Specifically, this relates to how good your HR service delivery is and what the real costs of providing these services are. There is also the question of the nature of the service offered and the balance in the type of work undertaken. If your intention is to shift from a transactional to transformational focus, it is a good idea to be clear at the start of your review on what the current balance is. Are you indeed loaded down with administrative tasks, leaving you little scope for strategic contribution?

Figure 2.1, shown earlier, indicated how organizations visualize this repositioning of the HR function.

QUALITY

What sort of data might be collected on service quality:

- Time taken to recruit staff?
- Time taken to appoint internally?
- Number of disciplinary/grievance cases handled?
- Proportion of employees who were appraised in the previous year?
- Number of onto and off payroll adjustments made?

This sort of data should allow an informed discussion of the service to date. It should indicate areas of strength and weakness. This should help later in terms of redesigning the HR function. If there is slow and inefficient recruitment service, this might justify the need for change. If, on the other hand, candidates are dealt with in an efficient and friendly manner that puts the organization in a good light, you might be much less inclined to interfere. Looking at data should have the added benefit of sizing the workload. This is important if the work is to be transferred elsewhere, be it to line managers or to a shared service centre. Sticking with the recruitment example, managers will need to know what they are letting themselves in for if they were to assume responsibility in place of HR. 'How many recruits does this typically mean?'

TYPE OF SERVICE

Your aim is to distinguish the type of work you currently do. This could be on a functional basis – how much effort is expended on reward, training and development, organization design, etc. But if you already have a functionally based organization you should know, through staff numbers in each function, what the balance of expended effort currently is. If you have many HR generalist positions, then establishing the extent to which they are working on pay, resourcing, performance management issues, etc. can help when you are thinking about future design. It will enable you to decide on staff numbers, but also to give you a steer on what sort of skills you need in your of centres of excellence or consultancy roles, should you require them.

Organizations are often less concerned with the functional split and more interested in uncovering how HR colleagues spend their time from a value-added point of view. By this we mean, how much time is being devoted to administration, how much to operational support, how much to policy or strategic development and in what way does the balance of task shift by job. Naturally, you would expect a personnel service assistant to spend much of their day on administrative activities. It would be more worrying if an HR manager was doing a lot of work helping to sort out relocation expenses, company car purchase or pension entitlements.

EXAMPLE 4.3

BOC UK wanted to shift the balance of its HR workload from administrative to strategic. They undertook an activity analysis that showed that 27 per cent of HR time was spent on strategic issues, 41 per cent on the delivery of HR issues, and 32 per cent on administration. They compared these figures with other BOC Group companies and found that the UK was not in bad shape internationally within the group. However, the aim was to shift more towards the strategic and away from the administrative.

Data to permit this sort of analysis can be collected via:

- staff being asked to keep a diary
- using detailed timesheets
- high-level assessment, review of calendars
- tracking the number and content of:
  - telephone calls
  - emails
  - personal visits
  - correspondence.

To be able to get a comprehensive and accurate account of time spent, you need the co-operation of your HR colleagues. It is very easy to sabotage such an exercise, so you have to position the exercise carefully. You have to explain why the review is being conducted and the purpose for which it is used. You will probably have to assure people that analysis will not be done at an individual level but, say, by grade and function. This assurance is obviously more difficult to give in a small department. However, the point of the exercise is indeed to see what work comes in and is not for the purposes of assessing the performance of individuals. You can argue that staff are rightly responding to the current demands of customers. The aim of changing the HR function may be to reconstruct this relationship in a different way.

COST

If the main driver for the introduction of HR shared services is to reduce overall HR costs, it is vital to properly assess what these are before the project commences. This is important because HR costs often have not been well tracked in the past and expenses may be hidden from view. Not only will this provide good metrics for measuring the impact of any change you propose (e.g. reduction of HR costs at 20 per cent may be be affected by a number of factors), it will also ensure that the shared services function does not underestimate the people and financial resources needed to at least maintain service at current levels.

There are a number of variations in the method of assessment you could use, including:

- high-level assessment of the number of full-time equivalents (FTEs) undertaking the target work under review. Cost is then apportioned: e.g. 10 staff distributed across function input data and nothing else. Payroll costs are £25 000 per head, inclusive of all on costs. Therefore total cost is £250 000 fully loaded.
- activity value analysis is a more detailed look at the costs drivers and outputs. It is used to establish the cost of each activity: e.g. to undertake each maternity case costs £300 per employee. There are 100 cases per annum. Therefore the total cost is £30 000
- detailed activity-based costing where the total HR function costs are apportioned across a pre-defined activity 'dictionary': e.g. the total time spent on recruitment is £5 million, split into attraction, selection, administration and induction.

The same sort of methods used for discovering how time is apportioned, reported above, can be used for establishing cost.

Some organizations are able only to perform these calculations within the scope of the HR department. More recently, we have seen in the higher profile outsourcing deals, most notably BP, total input costs including line management time being calculated.

These activity-based exercises are also useful for measuring how HR is spending its time. Whether it is, for example, meeting its strategic objectives or spending disproportionate energy on administration.

Done well, activity (value) analysis reviews can be highly effective, however the methodology comments discussed in step 2 are critical to ensure that the exercise is not seen as a 'big brother' tactic. It is also critical to ensure that the level of accuracy and input to the data is robust.

PROCESS

You need to look at your HR processes. How are they put together? Do they link well? Are they integrated into an end-to-end view of the employment event – from hiring to retiring? Figure 4.2 illustrates the sort of process map you might use. This is important since organizations grow and change over the years, and structures and processes may not fully adjust to the change. So a tendency over the years to decentralize services may have created a patchwork quilt of delivery mechanisms, different in each business unit. Some organizations seeking to introduce shared services would deliberately centralize first and then streamline processes. They might conduct an activity-logging exercise where HR staff log all incoming and outgoing communications – be it by phone, email or face to face. This will allow analysis to be made not just of the level of activity (see Setting the numbers, p.48, for its use there) but in the connections between them. Improvement can then be made to achieve more efficient links. Re-engineering would be complete when the management information is aligned with the new process map.

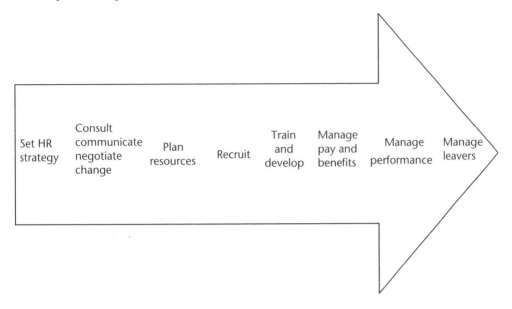

Figure 4.2   Process mapping in HR

Source: Carter and Robinson (2000)

This process map may allow you to focus on the areas that need most attention. For example, these are likely to be those of high impact on the organization where current performance is relatively weak.

Step 5: Establishing the capability of current HR staff

It is likely that in your revised model of HR, new skills will come to the fore and others will need to be seen at a higher level than in the past. Customer service and interpersonal skills are likely to be required across the board in your more client-focused operation. Contract and relationship management will be necessary if work is outsourced and/or managed via SLAs. Change management and strategic thinking skills will be needed by those expected to up their game and add more value to the business.

Before designing the shared service operation, or indeed concluding that it is the right route to go down, it is worth checking on the capability of your current staff in relation to these new skill demands. This is partly, as with the last section, to take a view of how their skills meet the current work demands, but it is more to do with how they might handle future challenges. Why is this an important question at this stage? It is always good to know at any early point the size of the change that might be required. This may simply be a case of understanding the implications of the transition, the cost and time required, but more fundamentally it may steer the design in a particular direction. If your capability review, for example, indicated that the computer skills of your personnel team were weak, then you would be ill advised to design a service delivery approach which relied heavily on computer networking, at least without factoring in either a substantial training or recruitment programme, or a combination of the two. You might choose, in these circumstances, to delay an automated approach until the skills' investment has borne fruit. Because of recruitment or retraining options, lack of capability in the HR team is more likely to impact the timing and cost of introducing change rather than prevent your organization eventually from getting your perfect design. Yet thinking about those who have to deliver the change is a necessary reminder that however brilliant a concept is in theory it nevertheless has to be capable of implementation. Some organizations have tended to neglect this fact.

So, what sort of capability review would seem appropriate for HR managers?

- How much are they doers rather than thinkers?
- How good are their influencing skills?
- What ability do they have in change management?
- How able are they at managing and monitoring third party relationships?
- Are they likely to be responsive to customer needs?
- How strategic is their contribution?
- How much are they business people – do they understand its language?
- How adaptable to change are they?
- What is their area of expertise at present, and from the past?
- What potential do they have for promotion?
- What has their past performance been like?

And what sort of capability review for other HR staff?

- What are their interpersonal skills like?
- Are they likely to be equally good or better in face-to-face, telephone or electronic inter-actions?
- How customer focused are they?
- How specialist is their knowledge?
- How adaptable to change are they?
- What is their area of expertise at present, and from the past?
- What potential do they have for promotion?
- What has their past performance been like?

For specific roles you would want to see particular skills. For example, considering candidates for centre of excellence roles you would want to see technical expertise; for jobs in a consultancy pool you would need competencies in creativity, facilitation, the ability to challenge, and so on.

The sort of skill sets that HR staff will require is affected by other aspects of the change programme. If, for example, introducing shared services is accompanied by substantial devolvement of HR activities to the line, this will require HR staff to act in a supportive role putting greater demands on their influencing skills. If a matrix organization is launched at the same time, then their ability to network will come to the fore. Creating business units may require HR staff to be able to balance corporate and operational responsibilities.

Such skill or competency information may be available from existing sources such as from appraisal forms. It may have to be gathered for this purpose, though, from interviews with senior HR staff and customers. A specific framework may be used, created to assess HR competency. This material may be collected by the HR director, the project team or outside consultants. A review such as this will give you useful data in determining what approaches to HR organization would be possible with the current staffing and reasonable levels of training. It can be used again after the design stage to give an idea of the resourcing and training implications of a new model. To be fully useful it would have to be supplemented by factual data regarding the HR team, such as:

- number of staff
- their location
- age, length of service profile
- grade profile
- technical expertise (as, for example, professional pensions administrators or trainers).

This data should help you look at the resourcing issues that different change scenarios present. Exiting a particular location may be easier if the age profile of your staff indicates that many will be retiring in the near future. You may find you have too few HR managers for new roles as business advisers, pointing to the necessity of recruitment. You may have the right number of staff but with the wrong skills. Hard, factual staff data enable you to uncover these potential problems or solutions.

Step 6: Technology assessment and status

There are few shared services projects that will not need a technological assessment. This is obvious if you are going to invest in new kit – an HRIS or payroll for example. It is even more true with the development of the e-HR capability. Those newer shared services ventures that aim for a number of e-HR facilities have undertaken rigorous technology assessments. These help, too, in the debate about whether to make or buy. They can establish the size of any necessary investment and help in making a judgement on what skills will be needed to implement change. You can see whether you can manage this in house or whether it would be better to contract it out or choose an ASP solution. But, even when you are using existing IT, you may well be trying to integrate physically dispersed systems – not always an easy task. So you should check that the systems are compatible either to transfer data to a single core system or can work together if they remain in separate use. You are likely to unearth lots of little systems, especially databases, that are used for operational support. Look out for absence reporting, shift planning, resource management systems and suchlike. You need to decide whether having a common system would be both cheaper and more effective (as it might be for absence management) or whether a local solution better meets business needs (for example, a rostering system for a unique activity). Getting this decision wrong risks resentment of corporate interference.

So, a technology audit would cover:

- the variety of HR systems in use, be they payroll, records and information, resourcing, etc. These will normally be electronic but could also be manual (but capable of being dealt with electronically)
- what they cost to run and importantly what you include in your running costs. Do you include capital depreciation, user support, user time, etc.?
- user satisfaction, known problem areas
- how they are supported, including suppliers track record in supporting systems
- the extent to which systems have been customized. This is especially vital if you are integrating diverse systems
- upgrade/licensing costs given current program release usage
- the future requirements for your HR systems – records, payroll, training, etc.
- whether there is a need to integrate with other business systems, e.g. finance (e.g. for workforce costing), logistics (for purchasing), production schedules (if there is a resourcing component), etc.
- whether or not there could be process improvements
- how able they are to support new functions, especially with respect to e-HR
- how access would work to an intranet and what the penetration/usage would be
- what the outsourcing or ASP options are, their cost, complexity and benefits
- if e-HR is being contemplated, the extent of personal computer (PC) coverage either on individual desks or publicly available. This review should also test the skills and knowledge of actual/potential users.

This will give you an idea of the expense and difficulty of maintaining and adapting your present systems. It should show the present pressure points but also the future opportunities. It allows you to judge the advantages and disadvantages of various solutions. Thus it helps set what the development pathway might be. You are likely to want to invest in the applications that give you the best benefit at lowest cost, and certainly to avoid the opposite. Benefit depends, too, upon the preparedness of the organization to take up new systems, be they in HR, the line or among employees. This recognizes that it is people who use systems and they need to at least accept proposed innovations. It is important to establish user support before sizeable commitments to shared services (e-enabled or otherwise) are implemented. You do not want to be lumbered with expensive 'white elephants'. You may think that this is too timid an approach, but it is crucial that concerns are tackled before final decisions are made, not after the new systems are delivered.

You can also make a decision on outsourcing. This does not have to be an all or nothing decision. You can look at your core HR database, applications and web as separate entities. But you must ensure that connectivity issues between the systems and with potential third parties are properly scoped and understood before taking the decision to contract out.

Step 7: Design structure

This is when you make the big design decisions discussed in Chapter 3. This is the point where you might decide to outsource bits of your HR operation. (Because of its significance we devote a separate chapter to the process of outsourcing.) Or you might create an in-house profit centre. You might want your HR shared services to be integrated with other functions or to be kept separate. Another decision to be taken is whether your shared service centre is to be dispersed or run from a single location. You will have to settle on the activities to be undertaken by HR or by line managers, and those that can be done electronically by managers and employees without the need for HR involvement. Finally, you need to settle on your approach to job design and resourcing.

If you want to keep your activities in house, you need to get the shape of your proposal clear before you test with your customers at the next stage. If you want to outsource you will need to define the boundaries of work to be transferred.

Step 8: Test with customers, colleagues and management

Many of those who have designed shared service structure have admitted that they gave insufficient attention to the views of customers. The latter may have been involved at the initial point of the project, step 3 in our approach, but then have been presented with a *fait accompli* at the end. Other organizations have talked of the resistance of HR colleagues to proposed changes. The third group that you should not neglect is senior management as they will ultimately approve your plans. We suggest you avoid or minimize these difficulties through consultation with customers, colleagues and senior management after you have completed your draft design.

How effective consultation will be will depend upon your track record as a function. Are you seen as effective and responsive? Do managers and employees trust you? In other words, do you start the exercise with high or low credibility?

Consultation has to be meaningful. You may have clear ideas of where you want to get to, but you need to know that your customers not only support your objectives (which they may have signed up to in step 1), but also the detail of your proposals. To illustrate the point, devolvement of activities from HR to the line may be accepted in principle by line managers, but they may object to specific detail. They may prefer to leave certain tasks with HR or retain HR's involvement. This has happened with respect to recruitment. HR might see it as wholly appropriate that managers do their own recruitment, but the latter may value the contribution of personnel staff. And there may not be a consistently held view across the organization. Some parts of your organization may wish to complete autonomy from the HR function for hiring, and others may want to rely on HR to resource for them. Experience suggests that neither model is right, and a one-size-fits-all approach can lead to expectations not being met.

EXAMPLE 4.4

Differences of view over recruitment emerged in an engineering company. In HR's mind line managers would take full responsibility for recruitment. However, the managers themselves were less keen that they should be wholly responsible. They wanted HR to participate because they welcomed their expertise and independence. So HR went back to assisting with recruitment.

Consultation with HR colleagues can be trickier. They may not have subscribed to the change objectives in the same way as the line. They also are more directly affected – their jobs may change or even be lost. Emotion may be involved in their reaction to change, both in terms of the personal impact and in their view of the sort of service personnel should provide. It is therefore a matter of judgement as to on which issues there is to be genuine consultation and on what subjects it is more a case of selling the logic and benefits of a new approach. This may mean a distinction between advocating the strategy and direction of change whilst accepting useful input on the best way it is to be delivered. You need to decide on your strategy to deal with 'blockers'. Do you move out obstructive managers, as some organizations have done? Or do you work intensively on those with doubts, listening to fears and trying to bring them round?

EXAMPLE 4.5

Getting HR staff directly involved in the design of a new approach to service delivery was seen at the BBC. HR managers attended a simulation event at which the first cut model was identified. This was so successful that before going live other HR staff were invited to participate in 'jigsaw' meetings. Here there was debate about how the pieces of the design jigsaw should be put together. To test ideas there was role-play where HR staff tried out the newly constructed roles. Some line managers also attended business meetings. They joined in the role-play and were able to challenge design features and improve the emerging model. Employees were not specifically invited but HR staff played their parts to see whether their needs were being attended to.

This enabled the project team to see where there were links between parts of the HR function and where they were absent. This allowed a process map to be created.

Separately, the HR team developed a set of common processes, identifying best practice in how to deliver HR services. This facilitated training on a common basis.

Few organizations are likely directly to ask for employees' views, but employee representatives can be asked their view via a consultative forum. Some organizations would build this into their change management model, even before any formal requirement to consult (i.e. over redundancies or transfers). This has much to commend it. Designers of new service delivery models may make a number of assumptions regarding employee preferences that are ill thought through. For example, it might be assumed that all employees are happy to interact with the HR function electronically. Some employees may still prefer telephone, or even face-to-face communication for sensitive matters. The organization will have to judge how significant this group is and whether it is desirable or cost-effective to meet their needs.

For senior management, consultation at this stage should be seen as part of building the business case. In step 1 you should have obtained a commitment to the need for change and clarity over what senior management expects. You should know where the emphasis should lie in terms of cost reduction, improved service or organizational flexibility. At this point with a draft design in place, you should be testing to what extent your proposals meet their expectations and surfacing any concerns over your ideas. These might include worries about an overreliance on technology, doubts about whether line managers can cope with tasks transferred to them or insufficient support to individual businesses. Criticisms could be more strident – not enough cost is being taken out; greater outsourcing ought to be considered; the HR function is still too large and unfocused.

What form should this consultation with customers, colleagues and management take? If there is a customer panel it would be ideally placed to give an informed view. With line managers it may not be possible directly to consult each one. An alternative might be to send them proposals and invite their comments. However, most managers have a mound of paperwork and, consequently, another document in the in-tray may not get that much attention. Also a degree of explanation may be necessary and debate healthy. Thus holding a workshop might be a better solution.

As we indicated earlier, employees may best be consulted via their representatives in a consultative forum. An employee survey may be necessary if the proposed change is particularly radical. Otherwise, there may be a rather limited and ill-informed response.

Consultation with the HR team must engage all members. Depending upon the size of the group, this might be conducted in a single meeting or a series of meetings. It would be better if the HR director took a lead in giving the broad outline before his/her senior managers discussed the implications on their own area of activity. As the introduction of shared service may cut across traditional department lines, it may well be necessary to mix up the HR group and form temporary teams to look at different aspects of the plans. If these teams were led by a member of the change programme it might encourage 'out of the box' thinking rather than being constrained by current conventions.

A formal presentation is likely to be necessary for the management team. This will:

- confirm the objectives of the review, e.g. to position the HR function as a significant contributor to business improvement
- restate the reasons why it is being undertaken, e.g. to reduce expenditure on HR but simultaneously improve the quality of HR delivery
- specify the options considered and the preferred option, e.g. shared services is proposed rather than creating mini HR departments for each business unit
- indicate the benefits of the change, e.g. a 20 per cent reduction in HR costs but the introduction of standardized HR processes based on good practice within the sector
- clarify the risks of moving to a new model, e.g. possibility of new technology failing or of insufficient bespoke support to individual business units
- emphasize the fit with other business changes, e.g. the general move towards cheaper, more standardized services across the support functions of the organization
- specify any investment needs and how they will be paid for, e.g. in a new HRIS or employee self-service model.

The project team will then need to pull these inputs together, especially if they are provided in parallel rather than sequentially. Naturally, judgements will have to be made over what modifications to make to the draft design in the light of the comments. Where there are differences of view there may be a further consultation necessary to reconcile them. On occasion, the project team may feel it necessary to stick to their design in order to meet their objectives. This might mean rejecting criticism that a change is not achievable or is undesirable. Vested interests may have led to the position adopted, but even here the project team should go back to those they have consulted and explain why they have not accepted the objection. Another approach is to reflect top-down and bottom-up views. In this way ideas generated by users could be evaluated (but not dismissed) by the management team. Similarly, proposals by the management team could be evaluated by the project team in the light of user comments.

Step 9: Detailed role design

Having got the shape of the structure you wish to implement, you now need to add detail. A good starting point is to look at the high-level structure design and product offering. This should give you an idea of the roles required and key accountabilities that need to be established. It is critical to understand the extent to which processes are instigated by line management, interact with customer-facing HR teams and establish whether the interaction is directly with the shared services function. In particular, this will give a strong flavour as to the balance of processing skills/customer service skills that the shared services functions require. From these processes you will have obtained a reasonable idea at the design stage of the roles you need; now you need to firm these up. Similarly, you will have thought about the number of jobs involved; again this needs to be confirmed. A helpful way of achieving these twin objectives, and of putting you in a position to fill the posts, is to specify the roles that will need to be performed.

EXAMPLE 4.6

Shell UK Exploration and Production identified four roles, two that sat within the shared services concept and two that were outside it. Inside shared services were:

- HR operations – the 'engine room' of HR that acts as the 'centralized processing unit for all transactional activities'
- consultancy services – a flexible pool of HR consultants to be called on as required, offering specialized services in such areas as organization development, reward, recruitment, training and development and employee relations.

The two roles outside shared services were:

- 'line partners', front-line professional HR advisers supporting change and developing strategy within their businesses
- corporate HR managers dealing with the organizational leadership team.

Some organizations will choose to do this by writing detailed job descriptions. This may help because the jobs will have to be formally evaluated and, therefore, written up in the proper format to enable this to be done. Job descriptions may also have to be written because employees expect to see this information as part of their formal contract of employment. In other organizations looser role descriptions are sufficient. Whatever the format, you will need to explain:

- the reporting relationships
- the principal accountabilities
- the main task/areas of responsibility
- the key deliverables.

In addition, even if not required for the job description, you should specify the personal requirements of the job:

- the knowledge, skills, qualifications
- experience/track record
- the behavioural competencies.

EXAMPLE 4.7

British Energy (IDS, 2001) defined the skills it required for its shared services staff as follows. They had to have:

- communication and interpersonal skills – written and verbal
- computer literacy
- customer focus
- numerical facility
- organizational and administrative skills
- accuracy and compliance to standards.

It was also helpful if they had got previous experience with relevant software, a helpdesk facility and the HR activities they would work in.

BOC had similar requirements. It emphasized focus on the customer, what he/she wants and needs, and a desire to deliver a high-quality product.

PricewaterhouseCoopers (PwC) recruitment to its shared service centre looked to broad customer skills as much as professional know-how. This is because the HR component is built into processes that the staff administer. So, for example, PwC employs an ex-customer service manager from McAlpine Homes and an ex-mortgage adviser from NatWest. (Arkin, 2001)

Whether it is based on a formal job evaluation or not, the grade, pay range or salary level will need to be set.

Before looking at the candidates to fill these posts, it is worth looking again at the structure you have produced based on the detail of the roles you have created. You might ask yourself:

- Have managers been presented with too wide a span of control?
- Do specific jobs overlap too much?
- Are there gaps in organization where work may fall through the cracks?
- Is there too much duplication of effort in some areas? Have you over-resourced altogether or provided too much resource in some areas and insufficient in others?
- Are the jobs doable by normal human beings in terms of the skills required, the breadth/depth of the role? This should refer back to your broad design choices covered in Chapter 3 concerning whether you want more generalist or specialist roles (or vice versa).

It may be obvious to the reader, but even in an outsourced model the importance of describing the scope of the key internal roles (more based around supplier/financial management than operations management) is just as relevant.

Step 10: Formal consultation with employee representatives

Depending upon how you structured your project team in step 2, you may have involved employee representatives in the project from the start. Alternatively, you may have kept them informally aware of the progress of the project as it has proceeded. It is unlikely that you will have left local trade union representatives or staff consultative committees in the dark. Springing change on people without preparation is a recipe for generating resistance. Now that you are clear on the approach you are going to take and the implications of what you intend to do, it is timely to consult employee representatives formally. This is especially true if you believe that there will be a surplus of staff compared with future requirements, thus with the potential of redundancies. This may then produce a legal requirement to consult. Similarly, if you intend to outsource services then you are obliged to inform and consult.

What is legally required in relation to outsourcing is discussed in Chapter 5. Consultation on redundancy is broadly similar to consultation with respect to transfer of work, but the content of the consultation is necessarily different. It should be recognized that at the time of writing (late 2001) further changes to the consultation on redundancy is being considered.

Beyond fulfilling your legal obligations, the extent and nature of the consultation will depend on how radical your plans are, how big the impact is on employees and the nature of employee representation. If you have an agreement with trade unions, then this will indicate what you will need to cover and probably when and how. Irrespective of your obligations it would be good practice to explain to employee representatives the sort of issues we covered in step 8. This means setting out the rationale for change and indicating the implications on numbers, roles, location, etc. You should give the representatives the opportunity to comment. This means building time into the process for them to reflect on what you have told them and to respond. Clearly, a judgement will have to be made if they come back with critical comments. You need to decide whether to modify your approach, change elements in it or ignore what you have heard because you think it is merely a defence of the status quo. However, it is worth keeping your ears open because the representatives may point to practical problems with your design that you had missed or give good advice on how implementation might be improved. You would be foolish to ignore genuine concerns or to discount good ideas.

EXAMPLE 4.8

Shell UK Exploration and Production held meetings with their 'staff committees' at an early stage in their HR review. The project team chose to inform and consult immediately after talking to the HR community and at the same time as line managers. All staff were communicated with immediately afterwards.

Conclusion

So, to summarize, you need to:

- gain senior management's commitment to change
- establish a project team and decide your approach to managing this change
- obtain the views of your customers on the service they have had and the service they would like
- verify the current standards of your HR service. Find out where improvement is most required

- determine the capability of your current HR staff – what are they good at doing? Where does their experience and expertise most lie? Where are the knowledge or skill gaps?
- establish the position of your technological infrastructure. What systems are in use? Which ones link together and which stand alone? Which give problems, which work well?
- design your preferred approach
- test your ideas with the customers/stakeholders – employees, line managers and senior management
- finalize the design of jobs and the number of staff required
- formally consult employee representatives over your proposed changes.

5 *The process of outsourcing*

Outsourcing is an option for you to consider in relation to some or most (probably not all) of your HR services. A successful outcome to this process requires that you are clear as to why you are doing this (what benefits do you seek?), finding a suitable provider, settling upon the right sort of contract, determining the correct procedures to manage the contract and transferring the work/people in an effective manner. This chapter will consider these issues.

How do you decide whether to outsource?

So how do you decide whether to outsource HR services? On what basis do you choose?

One way is to consider a cost–benefit analysis under which you might keep work in house or contract it out. This might consider the following issues:

- Using external suppliers tends to be cheaper where the service to be performed is widely available (e.g. training or payroll services) because competition keeps down the costs and suppliers can achieve economies of scale.
- Using external suppliers gets more expensive the more unusual the service is, the more bespoke it has to be or the less frequently the service is required. This is because it is expensive for a supplier to gear up to supplying a unique service.
- Monitoring costs have to be borne in mind. They tend to be higher for the more complex operations.

Another approach is to establish a set of criteria to determine where outsourcing might be appropriate. It might be chosen where the services:

- are resource intensive
- are discrete, i.e. can be easily separated from the rest of the organization
- are specialist in nature and rarely performed
- are irregularly required making resourcing decisions difficult
- where there is a mature external market
- are subject to rapid technological change making it expensive to keep up to date
- where it is difficult to supply labour (costly or difficult to recruit, train and retain).

A third way of looking at this is to analyse your core business areas or core competencies to determine what you retain and what you outsource. An example used by one organization is shown in Figure 5.1. This uses a core/non-core distinction together with a supply indicator: is there a ready supply of labour with the requisite skills or an absence/shortage? Thus if the activity is core then outsourcing would only occur if it was difficult to carry out the work in house because of a shortage of skills. This still begs the question of the definition of the core and how it is arrived at. Some organizations would use the type of criteria listed above. Other organizations may make a more considered judgement on those activities that are thought to be the source of its competitive advantage and those that are not. Yet this, too, requires further analysis as it is by no means immediately apparent what provides competitive advantage.

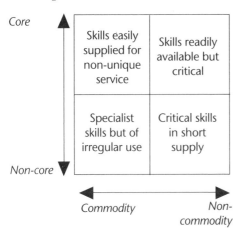

Figure 5.1   Analysis of core business areas and labour supply

Source: Reilly and Tamkin (1996)

Whichever approach is taken you should make the decision in a systematic way, to reduce the chances of encountering the problems described later. The more sensitive or critical the item is to the organization, the more a proper strategic review is necessary. This should draw out implicit assumptions behind your decision. It allows testing of your views with colleagues and against other options. You should acknowledge that outsourcing is but one possibility to improve productivity and reduce cost, but it has advantages and disadvantages compared with other options that need to be evaluated. If you do not identify the cost/benefits of the chosen route in advance, it will not be possible later to scrutinize whether the benefits have in fact been realized.

A proper evaluation would take account of:

- clear corporate objectives setting out the requirements of the exercise be they cost reduction, service improvement, expertise acquisition, etc.
- a risk assessment which considers the technological and business implications of change
- consideration of security and confidentiality issues which may constrain choice
- a full estimation of the cost/benefits, including the non-financial, e.g. skills impact, or cultural effect, to be done on a long- as well as a short-term basis
- whether and how the activity links to other core processes
- an evaluation of the market to see if there is sufficient competition of the requisite quality to keep costs down and quality up
- whether the same objective could be met internally by relocating activities and/or staff, or by redesigning jobs or processes
- whether HR activities could be managed by a separate cost or profit centre, possibly as a subsidiary company
- whether the alternative external routes, such as via a management buyout (MBO) or joint venture, might be appropriate
- an assessment of the cost of retaining activities in house in terms of human or physical resources
- consideration of tax, legal and procedural issues which may inhibit or alter the decision to outsource.

The sort of decision-making process we envisage is illustrated in simplified form in Figure 5.2.

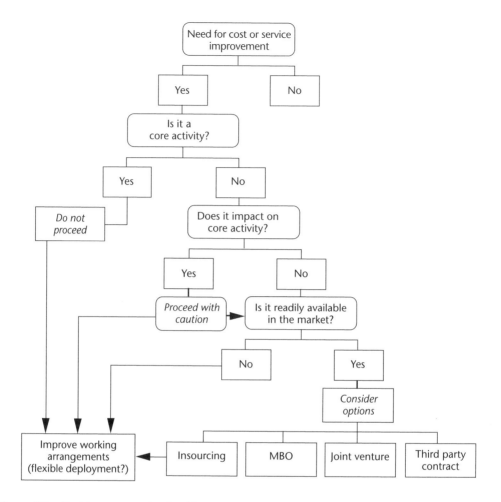

Figure 5.2   Decision tree on who should execute HR activities

Source: Reilly and Tamkin (1996)

The word 'core' in the model in Figure 5.2 can be substituted by 'critical activity' or 'source of competitive advantage': the point is to distinguish between those areas where a high degree of internal management control is seen as necessary to protect a vital interest and those activities where the risk of service failure is less or the cost of failure lower. Determining whether the activities you currently undertake are part of your core business, requires you to define criteria on which to make a judgement. These might include:

- uniqueness of resources, be they skills or physical assets, systems or structures
- providing critical differentiation with competitors and market advantage
- whether the activity offers added value
- the nature/size of invested assets
- whether it is part of operational integrity
- the relationship to the brand
- the risks to the viability of the organization if not properly performed.

To give an illustration of this thinking. Planning the succession of senior managers can be viewed against this list as follows:

- The resources being considered may be unique, but the skills to carry out succession planning are not. There are no physical assets involved, but systems or processes may be bespoke.
- Succession planning may not be providing critical differentiation with competitors and market advantage as a process, but its outcome could do. Top managers will not join your organization because they like your succession planning process, but the process may be better at uncovering talent compared with your competitors.
- Succession planning does offer added value. It should identify future gaps in the organization, take steps to fill these gaps and develop those with talent to come through in the future. Done well this could make a difference to the success of your organization.
- There are no invested assets in the succession planning process.
- It is part of operational integrity. Indeed in the financial services sector it is a regulatory requirement.
- Succession planning has no direct relationship to the brand, but the outcomes may be related to it. The City in particular looks to see whether a firm is well managed, and succession planning can be argued to be an integral part of key people management processes.
- There are risks to the viability of the organization if succession planning is not properly performed. Having insufficient management talent can seriously prejudice the performance of the organization.

So, succession planning can be regarded as a core activity not because it is necessarily a unique process (though it can be), but because it is vital to the functioning of the organization. Could it be carried out by a third party? Yes it could, but it is integral to the management process and would be difficult to hive off. There is also the question of the confidentiality of the information that your organization, rightly, will be sensitive about.

By comparison, an assessment of training delivery as a core activity might look like this:

- Training may be unique only in the sense that some of material used may be particular to that organization. There are generally no specific resources (unless there is unique content knowledge), systems or structures.
- Training may provide critical differentiation with competitors and market advantage in areas where it has developed a bespoke approach. Potential recruits may be attracted by the extent and quality of the development offered, but may not be so fussed about the delivery mechanism.
- It should offer added value otherwise it should not be undertaken.
- They may be invested assets in terms of training staff and physical facilities. These may be separately organized in a training centre – making them easier to detach – or more integrated into the business.
- It may be part of operational integrity, especially if the training relates to health and safety or other statutory requirements, or relate to specific business deliverables.
- It may have an indirect relationship to the brand. For example, an organization with a well-trained sales force may reinforce the brand's position as one of integrity, reliability and efficiency. However, this does not mean that the delivery of this training has to be done in house.

- There are risks to the viability of the organization if training is not properly performed in the key areas noted above.

As you can see, training delivery is more complex than succession planning in establishing whether it is a core function. Some training is vital to the integrity of the organization and may well be regarded as such even though the actual process of training might not be unique. By contrast, other training is neither vital to the organization's survival nor difficult to replicate externally.

In thinking about these issues you should consider them over both the short and long term. This would suggest that some scanning of likely future developments is desirable. What is core is likely to change over time and greater caution is needed where the picture is complex or unclear. The greater the future uncertainty the less attractive outsourcing will be. Certainly, if a new activity is being considered, the criteria will have to be applied more carefully. Some companies take the view that experimentation is better managed externally, whilst others would argue that the benefits of learning are thereby lost.

Determining the contract strategy

Having decided to outsource an activity the next step is to decide your contract strategy. This helps you decide what sort of provider you are looking for, how you decide on your choice and broadly the nature of the contract you want to let. With respect to shared services there are three main options as to type of supplier:

- You could choose an organization with particular expertise in a field of HR (e.g. reward or recruitment). This obviously suits those situations where specific activities are outsourced rather than substantial chunks of HR work. Here you can benefit from the process and content knowledge of the provider.
- You could opt for an organization with technology as its prime offering. This suits organizations wanting to put in new payroll or records systems, employee self-service or web-based interactions. This option is particularly attractive where the technology is expensive, leading edge or complex, e.g. where certain e-HR solutions are being pursued.
- You could select an organization with broad based capability that can offer sufficient technological expertise (e.g. to run payroll and records systems) whilst at the same time offering support to handle a variety of people problems. This route will appeal to smaller-sized organizations.

Which sort of supplier you use thus depends upon:

- how selective an approach to outsourcing HR activities you seek, and which activities you want to contract out
- whether HR is acting alone or whether you choose to outsource HR in combination with other support services
- the extent of technological investment.

You then have to decide:

- whether single or multiple suppliers are appropriate. This, of course, will be affected by the range of activities being outsourced. Nevertheless, some organizations would opt for bundling their HR work together so that one company takes responsibility for the lot or giving specific activities (recruitment, training, benefits, etc.) to specialist firms. Partial outsourcing may also be chosen to test the capability of the contractor or provide a point of comparison between in-house services and an external supplier. This is most appropriate where the outsourcing market is undeveloped. This might be done in training services – outsource the generic work, but hold back on your bespoke training either to challenge your in-house team to improve or to test the capability of the supplier.
- whether to complete a partnership or transactional deal. This is again affected by the type of work under consideration. The more cost is the prime driver, the shorter the contract is likely to be and the more transactional is the deal.
- whether the assets and staff transfer or remain, and whether the service is to be on site or not. The retention of staff or equipment may be self-evident. In the case of resource-intensive activities with little equipment, such as recruitment, only the relevant staff would transfer. If you are requiring the contractor to provide the technical equipment, e.g. a payroll system or HRIS, then again there are no physical assets to transfer. But some outsourcing involves the use of the organization's own systems: the contractor operates them on your behalf (e.g. a records system). This may mean a contractor system on site or remote from it. A call centre is more likely to be off site when contracted out. Where consultancy services are outsourced then it would be possible for the contractor to operate remotely.

This then sets the broad framework for the contract specification.

EXAMPLE 5.1

Lincolnshire County Council decided to award its contract for all its support services (including HR) to a single bidder. It wanted to have just one provider because of the way the HR systems and processes were linked together. It also made contract management that much more straightforward. From the bids it received, it was evident that the council could simply replace its management by that of the contractor, but with limited change in approach, or it could choose a supplier that would change its processes. It opted for the latter. (IDS, 2000)

How best to manage the outsourcing process

You have chosen to outsource and have decided on your contract strategy; now you have to manage the process. Many of the elements are common to the process of introducing shared services, indeed to any complex change management process. You need to secure senior management commitment to the approach and agreement on the reasons why it is being undertaken. The next step is to appoint a project team that will produce a plan to effect the outsourcing, with a realistic timetable to achieve a successful outcome. In your team you should involve a number of parties:

- current HR service managers to provide understanding of the service, advise on standards and to deal with staff issues

- future HR service managers (if different) to ensure they grasp the cost, quality and contractual issues
- financial staff to ensure a full costing of the service is made, especially such hidden costs as overheads
- procurement or contract managers because they may well carry out the negotiations
- end-users of the service to ensure that proper service levels are set
- legal advisers to cover contractual (particularly in determining whose terms of business will be used – preferably your own) and employment law issues
- HR staff in their professional capacity for employee relations' advice and as key players in the communication and consultation processes
- public relations people to deal with media enquiries, particularly since outsourcing can be widely reported, especially in the trade press.

For your team to work you should have effective procedures, clear allocation of responsibilities, excellent communication and well organized co-ordination.

Your project plan should include:

- drawing up a specification for a contract
- determining a basis upon which to select contractors who will be asked to tender
- inviting competitive bids from suppliers on both price and service
- evaluating the bids on predetermined criteria
- awarding the contract
- setting up management processes to monitor and control its performance.

To most readers this would be obvious, but it is a sobering thought that some organizations do not invite competitive tenders for HR work and still do not operate even with a basic contract. This may be out of naivety – they do not expect problems – or because they trust the other party and so do not feel the need for any formal arrangements. Whilst it is true that in a partnership deal, you want a high degree of trust, it is prudent to recognize that, even with the best of intentions, things can go wrong. Unforeseen problems may occur that will need to be dealt with. To anticipate that there may be difficulties and to offer a means of handling them suggests that you require an appropriate contract. But before you get to that stage, it is advisable to properly test the market and see what different organizations might offer you.

We will look in more detail at the areas which you should cover to complete the outsourcing process.

SPENDING TIME ON THE TENDERING AND ASSESSMENT PROCESS

It is critical to have a clear contract specification, defining the scope of the work, before you invite bids from suppliers. This may be easy for well-defined areas of work, e.g. the relocation or counselling service. It is less straightforward where there is a close relationship with an activity you will retain. For example, you might choose to contract out recruitment administration but keep in house the attraction and selection processes. But is it clear where one ends and the other begins? Where are the interrelationships between the two? What work is handed over by whom to whom and at what point? These questions need to be answered in enough detail so that the work can be priced.

An alternative approach may be chosen where the activity to be externally undertaken is new. Here the bidders may be invited to propose the service they would provide. This gives scope for companies to offer imaginative solutions. A call centre may be designed in a number of ways and you should encourage contractors to come forward with their ideas.

In order to judge whether the bids are acceptable, you need to have a detailed understanding of your current costs against your present service. Otherwise it is hard to judge the quality of what you are being offered. Documentation also should be in a form that makes comparison between bids easy to make. This again requires clarity in service standards, but also on whether staffing levels, minimum wage rates, etc. will be specified. This will mean that a judgement will have to be made on whether TUPE applies or not; although the default position should always be that it does.

When it comes to selecting the contractor, clearly the price and service offered will be key criteria, but the decision is also likely to be influenced by their reputation, track record, your own experience (if any) and the contractor's apparent financial stability. It may also help your assessment by understanding the motives of the contractor – why do they want the business? Where do they expect to make the money?

DETERMINING THE CONTRACT LENGTH

One specific issue to be faced is what sort of contract length is appropriate. Clearly the sort of work involved is critical. Short contracts are more appropriate for cost-driven approaches to contracting and tend to be favoured for lower-skill or less complex tasks. These might be suitable for an activity like relocation services where there are a number of similar providers and a relatively straightforward activity. It can also be easily detached from other activities. Longer contracts are more appropriate if the handover time is significant and the contractor needs a long learning period; in other words, for work in more complex areas. This is favoured where there is a wish to develop a 'strategic alliance' or partnership between the client and contractor. However, if the latter route is chosen, optimal flexibility in the contract must be built in because the price to be paid for full flexibility is likely to be excessive. Failure to allow for changes in technological improvement or cost reduction can be expensive. It is difficult to predict where costs and technology will go over a 10-year period, but contractors tend to benefit the longer the contract. This is partly because discounts are often available in the early years, and partly because of increased efficiencies as the contractor gets to know the work better and a consistent income stream has financial advantages in itself. This analysis has discouraged some organizations from entering long-term contracts. Others have made contractual provision for changed circumstances.

DEVELOPING CLEAR CONTROL PROCEDURES

This involves setting service levels and/or quality standards, ensuring you have the means to measure performance and establishing procedures for handling non-compliance. The form of performance monitoring is not dissimilar to that described in Chapter 7, that is to the way in which it is generally used by organizations tracking how well services are undertaken; it just has to be tighter with external provision.

Performance measurement can look at process improvements and end-result benefits. These can be addressed through a statement of key deliverables rather than methods, a subject that is better left to the contractor to define. The deliverables used might relate to volume, timing and quality of the output. These have to be buttoned down otherwise ambiguities will later become apparent. What can be specified will naturally vary with the type of work; a standard operation such as records' administration can be much more completely specified than an operational service where it is impossible to cover all eventualities. Likewise, quality can be more easily measured in certain circumstances, say, payroll accuracy than in successfully providing counselling. Thus measurement may vary from simple targets, to such things as customer satisfaction surveys or by benchmarking performance against other service providers.

The setting of standards should apply to both normal and abnormal service. For example, in a recruitment service, if 90 per cent of applications have to be acknowledged within two days, what happens to the other 10 per cent? Is there a minimum quality level spelt out? If not, the contractor can be on target even if applications are not acknowledged within weeks, so long as the 90 per cent level is reached.

To be able to specify to this level of detail, close working between those negotiating the contract (e.g. a procurement department) and the current service provider or future service manager, will be necessary. The views of end-users will also need to be taken into account.

EXAMPLE 5.2

BP uses measures on both process improvement and end-result benefits in its deal with Exult. These include speeding up recruitment times and cutting costs, but it also involves obtaining better staff retention.

Capita's performance at Westminster City Council is targeted on completing tasks within a specified period. These include:

- updating information on the HRIS
- sending out recruitment packs
- dealing with disciplinary cases
- handling absence cases. (IDS, 2000)

In dealing with the above issues, you should consider whether there should be any contractual rewards for success, or penalties for failure. Examples of the former include allowing the contractor to retain a proportion of the profits from hiring out facilities, sharing the savings made on service delivery or simply receiving cash payments if service levels are exceeded. In joint venture outsourcing arrangements there is the opportunity to benefit from the profits of the operation.

The way failure to comply with performance standards is handled varies. You can decide, as Westminster City Council does, that extracting payment from the contractor does nothing to improve the service, merely making it more difficult to fund appropriate, restorative measures. Or, you can take the same view as Lincolnshire County Council. It levies penalty charges if its provider, Hyder, fails to meet certain service standards. You would certainly want at the very least to have a fallback measure to cover the eventuality of a major service breakdown. Whether you feel the need to keep the contractor on their toes throughout the duration of the contract, using inducements or penalties, probably depends on the nature of the contract. A simple transactional service better lends itself to this sort of stringent monitoring than a long-term partnership deal.

Whatever the charging regime, a regular reporting schedule is necessary. This should include both indices of performance and regular progress meetings. Problems can then be identified and dealt with. If difficulties cannot be overcome, there should be escalation clauses in the contract to resolve disputes and, ultimately, notice periods for termination. This may seem unnecessarily negative, but it should be accepted that problems are likely to occur. It should also be recognized that contracts are not static. Initially, mutual under-standing has to be worked on such that there is knowledge of respective objectives; it is not something that comes automatically. Similarly, cultural and other incompatibilities have to be sorted out. As the contract proceeds, different conflicts may emerge, especially if the balance of power begins to favour the contractor.

Charging arrangements may be a simple lump sum payment, made on a monthly basis, such as to provide a call centre operation, or it might be on an itemized basis, e.g. £x for each individual trained or employee relocated. It could be a combination of the two – lump sum for the more predicable activities and per item of service where volumes are variable. So some charges may be per head, some per event and some per action taken. You may have to add complexity to lump sums to deal with potential variation. Thus management of a records system may assume a certain workforce size. If this changes significantly then the contractor might expect to receive a higher fee for supporting a bigger population, and you would want a reduction if employee numbers were falling.

EXAMPLE 5.3

BT is charged by e-PeopleServe under a number of headings:

- There is a basic charge for the provision of e-HR services based on employee numbers.
- To complete a range of standard tasks, e.g. completing management information, there is a per capita charge.
- Each training course that is administered is charged per booking made.
- Any other non-specified activity will be charged on an agreed basis. (IDS, 2000)

CARE WITH TRANSITION

Transition has to be managed with respect to ensuring service standards are maintained and with changes in organizational configuration. A balance between the two has to be struck, otherwise the focus can all too easily be internal and the needs of the external customer can be neglected. Nevertheless, employee motivation and commitment need to be maintained during such uncertain times.

An early issue which has to be confronted is when and how to communicate with the affected staff. There are two schools of thought. One view is to communicate as late as possible, to minimize the risk of sabotage, and only via the incoming contractor, who then has an early opportunity to state their case. This means that staff hear directly from their potential future employer who can address their concerns.

The alternative opinion is the diametric opposite. It argues that concerns over sabotage are exaggerated and precautions can be put in place to reduce the risk. The principal aims of the transition, it is felt, should be to gain employee support for the process and to minimize fear of the unknown. This, it is believed, will be assisted by early information which avoids rumours developing. This option also requires you to take an open approach and one which demonstrates your support for the transfer. You may feel that there is an obligation on you to hear your own staff reactions and to respond to them. It is not suggested that the vendor is excluded from participation, merely that in sequence this is a second order priority.

EXAMPLE 5.4

Lincolnshire County Council made great efforts to find out employee feelings about the bidders to run their HR operations. All staff were invited to presentations given by the competing companies. Then they were asked to complete a questionnaire on the competing propositions. They rated the bids under a number of headings such as employment prospects, terms and conditions, training and development, their approach to the work, etc. The chosen company – Hyder – was the staff's preference too. (IDS, 2000)

Of course, legal rules and local collective agreements on consultation will impact the timing and nature of how staff are informed, whatever your preferences may be. As far as applying the legal requirements for transfer are concerned, whatever the size of your organization, you are obliged to inform and, in certain circumstances (defined below), consult 'appropriate representatives' of 'affected' employees. The 'appropriate representatives' must be union representatives, where the union is recognized. They can alternatively be 'affected' employees elected by their colleagues, either specifically for this purpose or not. You must ensure that such elections are fair, held in secret and votes are properly counted.

To allow employees to be informed effectively, you must provide employee representatives with sufficient information 'long enough' before the transfer to enable them to carry out their duties. The law does recognize that there may be 'special circumstances' which may influence an employer's ability to meet its obligations, but the courts interpret these circumstances very narrowly. Under the TUPE regulations you must formally inform representatives of:

- the fact of the transfer
- its approximate timing
- the reasons for it
- the legal, economic and social implications of the transfer for 'affected employees'
- the 'measures', if any, the transferor 'envisages' they will take in connection with the transfer
- the measures, if any, the transferee envisages they will take in connection with the transfer, for those who will become their employees as a result of the transfer.

This means that either you, the transferring employer, or the transferee, must inform employee representatives of the implications of the transfer, if any employee, even a single one, might in any way be affected by it. This specifically includes any 'measures' (i.e. 'action, step or arrangement') either party 'envisages' (i.e. visualizes or foresees as part of a plan or proposal) taking.

If you do indeed envisage that you will be taking measures as a result of the transfer, then there is a further duty to consult as well as inform. Consultation with employee representatives must be: 'with a view to seeking their agreement to measures to be taken'.

Thus you are expected to enter meaningful discussions, both with respect to their timing and content. Representatives should be allowed to respond and any proposals made should be considered and reasons given if any employee representative proposals are rejected. However, in the final analysis there is no duty to agree. If the measures include collective redundancies then there is also a duty to inform and consult under the terms of the relevant legislation – terms which are not precisely the same as those for business transfers.

Those employees standing for election and those selected as representatives are given the sort of rights and protection usually afforded to trade union representatives; that is, not to suffer any 'detriment' by virtue of his/her duties and to have reasonable paid time off, and access to affected employees to perform his/her activities.

You should also note that at the time of writing (late 2001) further changes to the regulations on Transfer of Undertakings are being considered.

The main way for you to ensure successful operation during transition is to provide a suitable handover to the contractor. Again, the nature and complexity (which can be of size as well as of technology) of the work area will determine its length. Some of the service failures that organizations have experienced may have been caused by an inadequately managed transfer of responsibility.

EXAMPLE 5.5

BAE Systems kept employees informed of its outsourcing plans through using a video, focus groups, a brochure, a regular newsletter and an intranet site. (IDS, 2000)

Another aspect of transition is making sure that the operation continues uninterrupted. This is more likely to be a problem if you have many new staff working in the shared services centre or if you have changed to a new technological base. In particular, care has to be taken in the transfer of data. Data has first to be validated. Then either paper or electronic records need to be moved to the contractor and, in the case of electronic files, rechecked to see that the transfer has been effective. You should also ensure that data confidentiality and protection issues are taken care of properly.

MANAGING THE CONTRACT

Once the contract has been awarded you have to manage it. You should have defined control procedures and monitoring mechanisms, but contracts do not run themselves. You need to have sufficient staff to oversee the contract with enough expertise to deal with issues as they arise. Otherwise, you are likely to suffer in terms of service quality, rising costs or both. The sort of tasks that will have to be performed include:

- assessing performance against standards
- evaluating claims by the contractor
- verifying contractor bills
- dealing with changes to service specification
- handling extra contractual requests
- acting as an interface between end-user requirements and the service provider.

The latter is particularly important where there are multiple suppliers and the objective is to provide a seamless service. Contract managers need to know that the supplier is meeting the conditions of the deal in the eyes of the users as well as in the statistics they receive. This may supplement survey material produced by the contractors themselves.

EXAMPLE 5.6

At Westminster City Council, their own HR staff conduct spot checks to test how the contract is working. The contractor, Capita, issues a questionnaire to users of their services inviting them to comment on the quality of what they have received. There is also a quarterly review of service performance by the departmental contracts board and an annual check by the finance committee. (IDS, 2000)

To be able to manage contracts in this way requires skill and knowledge. Staff have to be aware of the technical aspects of the work, but also the capability of negotiating with the contractor. Even in partnership deals the contractor seeks to maximize profit, whilst you, the client, want to minimize cost. You may both agree that service quality is important, but that comes at a price and you have to decide who pays.

Conclusion

Outsourcing of non-core activities can be a very successful move for organizations to make, especially if they can obtain services at a lower cost or at a higher level of expertise. However, if the decision is ill judged, problems are likely to surface. Costs may rise, standards may fall or the organization may feel it has lost control over something it now sees as vital to the effective running of the business. Even if the decision to outsource was right, you may nonetheless end up with a poor or costly service. This chapter has been aimed at helping you avoid this situation. You need to get the outsourcing process right. This means defining your contract strategy, mobilizing the correct resources, successfully moving the activity to another organization and monitoring the service. Short-cutting this process is likely to end in tears.

6 *Implementation*

There are a number of aspects to implementation. The first is, do you go straight ahead and launch the shared services model in one go or do you pilot it, test it or phase it in stages? This should help you answer the question, how quickly do you, or can you, move to your new form of operation? Next you will want to communicate your plans to the various stakeholders. You will have to appoint those who will operate shared services. Training will probably be necessary and should now begin in earnest in preparation for the start of operations. Users of the services may also require educating on how they can be used. This is especially necessary if self-service elements or web-based facilities are involved. Establishing a monitoring framework is the final feature of implementation, but necessary if the service is to be kept on track.

Testing and phasing

Testing your shared services model can be done at different points in your process. You can, if you wish, pilot various activities in order genuinely to evaluate whether the approach you wish to take is viable. This can be done immediately after design. Testing though can, as we describe it here, be more concerned with ensuring operational integrity. You are not deciding whether to proceed with shared services, you are testing to iron out any problems. This might be done to test the robustness of the whole service or of particular activities. It might apply to physical infrastructure or operating procedures and processes. The idea is to capture knowledge and apply the lessons learnt when the system starts operating in earnest. This identifies the benefits being realized but the risks being run. Some organizations compile a risk register of potential traps that need to be avoided.

   Before going live you really need to ensure that any new technology works. It might be a new HRIS that has been introduced that you want to test, or it could be a call centre that is about to function, or an intranet. Whatever the system it ought to be tested in an operational environment first, and certainly before resources are stripped out. It might seem overcautious to run, say, a parallel paper system alongside an electronic one or the old HRIS together with the new, but a service failure can be extremely damaging if there is no manual back-up. Examples of this type of problem are described on pages 141–2.

EXAMPLE 6.1

The NHS shared services initiative includes introducing a common payroll and records system across the organization. With over a million employees, this is likely to be the biggest project of its kind in the world. Rather than implement it directly, it is being tested via one 'test' site and 15 pilot sites. The arguments given for piloting are:

- to test the validity of the strategy
- to allow planning of replication or growth
- to confirm costs and savings
- to design key processes
- to offer a learning experience
- to communicate the initiative
- to demonstrate evidence of change and modernization.

Self-service can also be rolled out incrementally from doing simple to more complex tasks on line. You may want to do this partly to test the technology, but partly also to build a culture where employees feel comfortable and prepared to use the facilities.

In a similar way, if you have redesigned your processes, you need to check that the new approach will work in a process sense. This might be connected to the technological investment. Thus in a call centre, your first representative will take the initial call but be under instructions to pass on more difficult queries to a second line representative. You need to test that this system works. A caller needs to get an appropriate answer from the right person. So you may be checking the script of the telephone phase and of the escalation procedures.

EXAMPLE 6.2

One organization decided to check out both how the technology worked and how its processes would cope with typical questions and problems. So it got its HR staff to undertake role-play of customers and service centre staff. This helped improve processes, but it also helped at a personal level. Individuals got a feel for what the job entailed in a safe environment. They realized gaps in their knowledge and areas where they needed to improve.

Siemens decided to pilot its employee self-service approach just within the 100-strong HR community to iron out any process problems. Testing within the function was a low-risk methodology that had the added bonus of making HR staff themselves more aware of the model before it went live within the rest of the organization. The feedback from HR staff was very positive about the concept. In addition, the trial highlighted issues concerning data security, data integrity and systems integration as areas of critical importance. The board subsequently endorsed the concept and the service is now being scaled up so that it can be used by over 8000 employees.

Similarly, if you have invested in, say, a combined payroll and information system, you should make sure that data is being passed swiftly and accurately enough to the person doing the data input. If you have asked line managers to pass this data on, then you should check that they know what is expected of them.

Deciding to phase your introduction of shared services approach can be done for a variety of reasons and in many different ways. Its purpose could be to deploy limited project resources in a manner that enables the transfer to go smoothly. Your aim could be to convince doubters that it will work and meet its objectives (be that cost reduction or quality improvement). If you are outsourcing your shared services centre, you might wish to ensure that the subcontracting arrangements are efficient and effective.

Another argument in terms of phasing is that most organizations do not have sufficient resource to support multiple locations or business units introducing shared services at the same time. This is even more true if the range of services is extensive or the work complex. Phasing can allow you to devote this limited resource to where it is most needed.

EXAMPLE 6.3

The BBC has phased the introduction of their HR Operations activity by business area. Work for News, Sport and World Service came first, followed two weeks later by Resources and the other limited companies. Another two weeks elapsed before the professional services joined. But, then given the Christmas break and complexity of their operations, the other businesses (e.g. Factual and Learning, Drama, etc.) did not join for another two months. This phased approach means that each business division is properly supported and that learning is transferred to assist the incorporation of the next cluster of business divisions.

More contentious is whether it is better to phase in your shared services approach so as to convince sceptics that the system will work rather than press ahead quickly to give little chance for objections to be raised. For example, Transco had to work hard to convince doubting line managers that the service would improve rather than deteriorate. This was despite the extent of support managers would be given by HR, albeit remotely. (IDS, 2001)

EXAMPLE 6.4

A financial services company has moved forward on a business unit and location basis. It started its shared services model by combining the administrative support for the one division in two locations. Three years later two other divisions were added.

British Energy phased its introduction by subject area. It adopted a three-stage approach. First, salary administration and recruitment administration were transferred to a service centre. This got employees into the habit of contacting the centre and made it familiar for other forms of later work transfer. More general personnel administration and training administration followed. In the final phase, training administration relating to individual power stations was transferred. (IDS, 2001)

IBM has switched work to its shared services centre in Europe country by country. This has built up the range of businesses it could support over a period of time. The concept had already been proved to work in the USA but applying the idea to a multicountry setting was different. There was the multilingual issue but even more problematic was the different employment environments that had to be supported. When the centre went live in 1998, the UK, France and Ireland were included. Over the next two years a further 14 countries were added. (IDS, 2001)

The arguments in favour of phasing in change rather than opting for a 'big bang' are then that:

* you are seeking to identify any glitches at an early stage and certainly before problems become critical
* it allows testing of processes and systems to take place before complete roll out
* it permits implementation resources to be concentrated.

The disadvantages are that you may create a feeling of a continuous drip drip of change. This may be irritating to the HR team and to customers. The latter may become confused for a period of time during the transition as to who is responsible for what. This is especially true if you phase by functional activity, e.g. payroll, pensions, benefits, each successively put into the shared service centre. The customer may want to deal with all three activities over a single issue (e.g. on employing a person beyond normal retirement date) and find dealing with different models of service delivery irksome to say the least.

Moreover, it may be harder to effect a cultural shift if that is your intention. The benefit of the 'big bang' approach is that it gives a natural break between the old order and new delivery model.

Those outsourcing some or all of their HR work also have the option to phase in the transfer of work to their contractor. This may make the contract formulation more difficult unless the work transfer is done in clear bit-sized pieces – location, business unit, activity. However, testing that the contract is functioning properly can be done after the contract is signed. As Example 6.5 shows, you can regard, say, the first year of operation as a transitional year so that operational or contractual problems can be sorted out. This is much easier if you have a 'partnership'-style contract. It is more difficult, but probably much less necessary, if your outsourcing involves simple transactional work.

EXAMPLE 6.5

BT and e-PeopleServe have agreed a 12-month 'verification' period. This enables the parties to check that the assumptions in their contract are correct and workable. This is especially important with respect to forecasted activity, the way the charging system works and the standard of service is being delivered. (IDS, 2000)

Phasing can be done on a:

- geographical basis
- business unit basis
- activity basis.

If you do not want to launch the whole shared service at one go, you might phase it in over a period, activity by activity. So, for example, recruitment services might be consolidated first, then bring together payroll, with benefits administration following later, etc. Each element can be properly supported and validated before proceeding further. Phasing can also be done geographically – locations or regions progressively adopting a shared service approach – or by business unit. If you launch by location or business unit this means the complete service is rolled out at the same time, giving the customers the full service from the start; whereas adding services progressively means you can concentrate on one activity at a time. Which approach suits depends upon resources, customers and design.

Timescale

If you are phasing in the work, then it is likely you will have a more extended time frame for introduction than if you go straight to operate shared services in total. How long the phasing will be will depend upon whether it is conducted over a wide geographical area (as with IBM) or over the range of HR activities. This may be the difference between several years or a few months. Similarly, if you choose not to outsource the bulk of HR functions, but to contract out specific work packages, this may be done progressively over a number of years.

EXAMPLE 6.6

Telewest Communications made their decision to launch shared services in April 2000. By July the service centre was in operation. The work then moved in monthly intervals so that the transfer was complete by the end of the year. The company moved quickly to 'ensure minimum disruption to the business' and to 'give less opportunity for barriers to be erected to delay its (operation)'. (IDS, 2001).

For those opting for a 'big bang' there is usually a desire to move quickly.

Communication

It is vitally important to communicate to HR staff and users of HR services what changes there will be to HR services and how they will be delivered. The HR staff themselves may have been engaged in the design or consultation phases of the project. So at this stage, all that may be necessary is to confirm the nature of the new arrangements, perhaps with more detail added. Some users, especially managers and employee representatives, may also have been consulted. But, inevitably, there will be many who will be hearing about your plans for the first time. You need to tell them:

- why the change
- what is involved
- what impact will be on them
- how soon it will happen
- what the next steps will be.

The level of detail contained in this communication will depend upon the nature and extent of change. If tasks are to be devolved to line managers, then the implications will have to be spelt out separately in a fuller format. Similarly, if self-service is to be launched, employees will need to know what they have to do. Some of this type of change may be so far reaching that communication only positions the outcome of the review; user training is where the detail is added. This is covered later in the chapter.

There is a variety of different media you can use to communicate:

- face-to-face briefing
- video
- message on an intranet
- email or written communication
- poster on a noticeboard
- booklet
- magazines.

Which method to use depends upon the nature of the communication. An email message or a letter can inform on the broad outline of change, a booklet can give details of who to contact and on what phone numbers. There may then be phases of communication, aimed at different audiences.

EXAMPLE 6.7

Shell UK Exploration and Production produced a magazine called *Expro HR News*. This was produced as a one-off bulletin. It set out:

- 'why change?
- what is Expro HR?
- what will these changes mean?
- the HR journey'.

It also contained descriptions of each of the HR areas, and accounts of the policy simplification and online HR projects.

   IBM produced a five-minute video of their AskHR service, held on their intranet. This followed complaints from customers around the EMEA region who rang their local HR team, only to find themselves talking to someone in the UK of a different nationality. (Pickard, 2000)

You might wish to sell the benefits of the change or deal with concerns.

EXAMPLE 6.8

The benefits of moving to a shared services model were presented to staff at the BBC as offering:

- a fast response to queries
- instant access to advice
- clear and streamlined procedures
- fair and consistent standards
- help to build skills
- clearer relationships between managers and staff
- a consistent approach to people management as you moved around the organization.

The concerns expressed by managers over the proposed introduction of HR shared services were also addressed. These included:

- loss of personal contact with HR colleagues whom they would never see
- lack of dedicated divisional support by HR
- lots of additional work dumped on them
- loss by HR of local knowledge
- the move from single to multiple points of contact
- not directly seeing the savings made
- physical distance – never seeing us.

Appoint staff

You now have the overall structure in place and have described specific roles. You have role or job descriptions and personal profiles from step 9. So now it is time to appoint the staff. From step 5 you will already have a good feel for the capability of your current HR staff. This should tell you:

- how many posts can be filled internally with little prior training
- those jobs where there are good internal candidates but substantial training will be needed before they take up their positions
- the roles where you will have no choice but to appoint external staff.

To an extent organizations are constrained by law and good employee relations practice from having a completely free hand in their resourcing decisions. You cannot simply dump the existing workforce and hire another, not unless you move to a new location.

However, organizations do vary in the degree to which they seek to refresh their current staff and hire in new ones. Those that want to see a high employee turnover at this point do so because they want new skills, a more customer-focused culture, a greater level of task flexibility, etc. Other organizations like to emphasize continuity in their service delivery and customer knowledge and familiarity. This type of organization wants to retain as many people as possible. The latter is easier to accomplish than the former. But if you do want change, then through the relocation of offices, the way in which you design your roles and the selection criteria for appointment you set, you can maximize your chances of getting in fresh blood. Beware, though, that this process can go too far, as the salutary tale told on page 48 indicates – there is a risk that your service quality declines before it improves.

EXAMPLE 6.9

At a financial services company the shared services team was staffed from existing people in the HR function. Those appointed kept the relationship with the old team, as continuity was important in management's view of service delivery. This was especially necessary since each group had its own quirks (e.g. different overtime and bonus arrangements). Keeping continuity helped smooth the process with customers and reassure staff. They liked having a single named contact and one that they knew. But since the start, there has been movement in the team so as to allow greater flexibility of deployment and to avoid too much narrowness in attitude developing.

In staffing their shared service centre, one organization drew its staffing from existing employees, supplemented by some recruitment. The latter was used to cover natural wastage, but also to cover those who did not wished to stay – either because they did not want/could not adjust to the new situation or to take opportunity of voluntary severance. (Some thought it was a 'good time to go'.) There was greater refreshment at more junior levels – wastage is higher there. For HR manager posts it was largely a case of working with the existing population.

Recruitment, especially for administrative posts, stressed customer service attitudes and skills: content could be added later. Personal computer literacy was vital – in this sort of work the keyboard is your 'pen'.

BOC wished to see some new faces in their shared service centre. In their selection managers preferred people with customer service skills rather than HR knowledge. They were helped by a number of people who did not like the jobs on offer – they were too different – and who chose to leave on severance terms. This gave space to bring in fresh faces. BOC's strategy seemed to work. Customer satisfaction ratings of the HR service increased.

IBM's experience was even more marked in the staffing transformation that occurred. When their service centre opened in 1998, of the 80 people employed, 65 were new recruits. Three staff transferred from elsewhere in Europe and 12 UK employees stayed put. To fund these positions, there were job cuts throughout Europe by means of redundancy and redeployment. (Pickard, 2000)

Whatever the resourcing strategy, there are different ways to go about the selection process. Some organizations would seek to have informal discussions with every member of staff at an early stage before any formal selection process. This should indicate whether employees are happy to stay or would rather leave the organization when the new structure is put in place, and, if they want to remain, broadly what type of work they would like to do – take new jobs in the shared services environment or remain in more traditional roles. Other organizations would calculate the number of staff surplus to requirements based on the resources needed to fill the new structure against the current workforce and would then offer severance to those that volunteered to be made redundant. The difficulty with this approach is controlling the process. Some may volunteer to leave whom you would rather keep, so you turn down their request, which might not be well received. Others whom you might want to go, do not volunteer. The difficulty is that people may volunteer for redundancy for the 'wrong' reasons. For example, some might prefer to jump rather than be pushed, without realizing that you never intended to push them. Others with a get-up-and-go attitude might choose to take the money in the certain knowledge that they will get an alternative position. People of this calibre might be precisely the sort of people you wish to keep.

EXAMPLE 6.10

At Guinness, when the central shared services team was set up some four years ago, it was made up of those who volunteered from existing activities – 'natural selection'. There were no job losses.

At BP (IDS, 2000), the creation of Exult had a major effect on those employees working in transactional roles. Depending upon the extent to which individuals were so engaged (and therefore their work would move to Exult) employees were offered the choice of:

- remaining in their current post
- being redeployed elsewhere within BP – to an HR post or another function
- joining Exult under TUPE transfer terms
- accepting redundancy.

Relocating work complicates matters further. If you intend to co-locate staff because of cost savings or to improve integration, you will probably be closing down HR units in other parts of the country. It may well be impossible to physically transfer staff (they do not want to move/you do not want to bear the cost) and so redundancies become inevitable and defined. You then have to decide whether you have sufficient of the right skills in the location where the shared service centre will be sited.

Similarly, if part of the HR portfolio is to be subject to outsourcing, then you may have a defined population who will transfer to the new operators. However, as in the BP case in Example 6.10, you may give a choice to your staff as to whether they want to stay with you, move to the contractor or resign. Only large organizations will have the ability to absorb redeployments or allow employees to opt out of the work transfer. However, the more individuals can choose their fate, the more co-operative they will be in facilitating change.

Thus your approach to appointing staff will vary depending upon:

- the extent of the numerical surplus
- the nature of the skills match between present and future needs
- whether there are changes in the location of work
- whether parts of the function will be outsourced.

The main aim, though, is to ensure that at the end of the process you have the right people in the right places as far as is possible. This will mean that you should recognize the distinct skill sets for different roles. This is not simply a question of level, but of type of work. Consultants need interpersonal and project management skills to a high degree. They probably require breadth rather than depth. Business relationship managers are similar, but even more generalist – knowledge that is 'a mile wide and an inch deep', according to one manager. They also have to be able to negotiate to obtain resources (if there is a consultancy pool) and see decisions through to implementation and beyond. Specialist positions are the opposite of consultants: deep expertise must be a *sine qua non* in a centre of excellence. Senior positions in a service centre will be managerial posts above all else. These differences mean that individuals are not interchangeable. Companies report difficulties in getting business relationship managers to undertake other roles because their own is seen as the best job to have. Filling these jobs from the service centre or specialist positions has been seen to be problematic. One shared services manager said to us that you pay for it later if you mis-appoint, especially to business relationship manager roles.

You will probably wish to minimize enforced (or even voluntary) redundancy as far as is reasonably possible for the maintenance of good employee relations and the minimization of cost. You will want to balance the benefits of bringing fresh blood with new ideas and experience with the need for organizational continuity – the knowledge of the organization, how it works, its culture and its people.

Whatever approach is taken before appointing people to positions, clearly you have to recognize that some individuals may turn down the job you have offered to them. This may be because they wanted an alternative position (the benefit of early informal discussions reduces the risk of this happening) or are still seeking redundancy. You have to be clear in your own mind about how you will deal with this situation should it arise, bearing in mind the legal position.

Another angle to consider is creating flexibility in your resourcing mix. This may be pushed upon you. Some employees may already work part time, reduced hours or on a job-share basis. Others may choose to adopt this pattern because of the reorganization, and you will have to decide how to respond to such requests. Alternatively, you yourself might see advantages in having various working-hour patterns where jobs do not amount to full-time hours. Similarly, you might want to employ a number of temporary staff on short-term contracts to ease your way into the new arrangements. These staff may have specific skills (e.g. technological) or may just provide additional labour. Or you might want to institutionalize workforce flexibility by always having, say, 10 per cent of the team as temporary staff, engaged through an agency. This may be the right approach with high-volume, low-skill work, where organizational knowledge is not essential.

Dealing with these issues in a way that minimizes employer/employee antagonism and maximizes mutuality is likely to achieve the most success (see Reilly, 2000).

Train staff

There are various stages in the move to shared service where training will be appropriate. Training may be necessary before people take up their positions. This may be so that they have sufficient knowledge to do the job. For example, they may need to know the maternity benefit or relocation rules before they offer advice. It may be that they have to improve their behavioural skills, e.g. their interpersonal skills in handling customers, or their technical skills, e.g. in operating the HRIS or call centre system. Whether there is this need for pre-start-up training should be part of your implementation plan – see above.

EXAMPLE 6.11

At JP Morgan HR staff used 'work shadowing' in their 'client centre' to allow people to understand the work. (Pickard, 2000)

At Guinness some retraining was needed at the outset of the shared services operation some four years ago. The training was less about technical matters, more about flexibility and customer focus.

The next stage of training should be induction into the work, especially for those either new to the organization or new to the work, or both. Knowledge about the organization, its HR policies/procedures and the role are obviously critical. This may need to be built up over time so that the employee can absorb the information.

EXAMPLE 6.12

Telewest Communications had a very high proportion of new starters when it launched its service centre. The company put its new staff through a structured training programme. This was conducted by HR advisers who led the three work teams. Each employee was given their own personal development plan. (IDS, 2001)

At Cable and Wireless there were three components to HR training for HR business partners:

- strategy and change implementation
- project management
- consultancy skills.

Training, however, can also occur whilst in post. This may be intended to hone skills or knowledge already present, or it might be to respond to gaps or weaknesses. These may be revealed after a performance review. It is a good idea to conduct an early review of how staff are getting on in their new jobs after six months. Any problems can then be tackled before they grow to be too significant.

EXAMPLE 6.13

BOC conducts reviews of its shared services staff after six and 12 months. Their knowledge is tested by being given 60 typical questions to answer, such as:

- 'What are the stages in the manual staff's disciplinary procedures and what time periods apply in each case?
- What are the qualifying rules to join the sharesave scheme?
- An employee wants to see their personal file – what is your response?' (IDS, 2001)

Training may also aim to develop staff to allow them to do higher-level work. For example, in structures that have different response levels, an employee could be trained to go beyond giving a factual response to a question (e.g. how many days compassionate leave are staff entitled to) to an interpretative answer (can compassionate leave be extended if there are specific extenuating circumstances?). Developing the role can include growing breadth as well as depth. Particularly in shared service centres where staff are organized as specialists, staff can be encouraged to broaden their area of knowledge for, for example, cover reasons. Thus somebody who covers employee benefits might be trained to cover payroll entries when other staff are sick or absent on leave.

EXAMPLE 6.14

Team meetings are used at a financial services company to spread knowledge and agree how to respond to non-standard issues or new problems. They have people with particular expertise in certain areas who are expected to impart their knowledge to other staff. Lunchtime team meetings are one way in which this is done.

Training has been an important feature of the introduction of shared services at the BBC. The involvement of staff in the design of the HR service has proved very helpful in gaining staff understanding. Further information on changed HR processes has had to be given uniformly across the shared services activity. Giving staff knowledge of the businesses they will support has proved necessary in HR operations as not everybody is working with a business segment they know from past experience. The business-facing HR partners continue to keep people up to date with developments across the company. Employees have been instructed in how to operate the new HR model.

Much has been achieved through the use of 'learning breaks' and lunchtime sessions to cover issues on the content of calls concerning HR policy and practice. Workshops have proved good at team building both for those working within the shared services activity and between them and the HR partners. Further training has been aimed at continuous improvement. This has emphasized using the new technology, business awareness and applying the redesigned processes.

Telewest Communications has used an 'e-room', a shared intranet site accessible only to HR staff. Here they can both obtain information on policies/procedures, but also post questions and receive answers on matters where they are unsure of the company's position. It's a kind of HR 'chat room'. (IDS, 2001)

Another dimension to training is to make sure outsourced staff are fully trained to do their work. The contractor should be responsible for all basic training, to ensure that staff are capable of doing their jobs. However, you will have to be certain that the contractor's employees know all they should know about the policies and procedures of the organization, how it works, how things are done round here. This is obviously critical the more technical is the work, and also the more integrated is their service with your own.

EXAMPLE 6.15

Those working at Hewitt Associates for the Royal Bank of Scotland (RBS) receive customer service training, accuracy coaching and information specifically relating to the bank. All calls are recorded. A proportion is then selected for analysis. This is then used in giving help to Hewitt's staff, either in interpersonal training or in dealing with HR issues.

Educate users

Communication can turn into training for users. Indeed, some mechanisms have this dual purpose. You can use workshops to explain what the changes are to HR before going on to describe what impact it has on managers/employees. The meeting could then become more instructive in terms of telling people what new responsibilities they have – employees logging skills data on the HRIS or managers conducting disciplinary interviews alone. A question and answer session can then pick up both comments and queries.

Some education may be simple, as in the Compaq example below, telling customers how to contact HR.

EXAMPLE 6.16

Compaq issued stickers and water cups with the following message:

Stuck with an HR query?

- The answers to most HR queries can be found on the HR homepage
- No luck? Speak to your line manager
- Still need assistance? Email us at ...
- Otherwise, call the HR service centre on ...' (IDS, 2001).

Where there is something to see, visiting the service centre might be helpful.

EXAMPLE 6.17

At JP Morgan they have a 'client centre'. Throughout the initial phase of operation, they have had visits and 'half day work experience sessions'. This is to allow them to 'educate' HR staff and customers in the work that is done there. (Pickard, 2000)

Other education is more detailed, setting out the rules of the game – as the BOC example shows.

EXAMPLE 6.18

BOC (IDS, 2001) produced a guide for line managers. It sets out who in HR to contact and why, e.g.:

* to change a salary, benefit, allowance, etc.
* to make an offer of employment
* to ask for a management report from the HRIS
* to inform when there was a leaver
* to clarify HR policies or procedures.

Where the introduction of shared services involves a switch of responsibilities from HR to the line, there is a requirement to do more. This means, at minimum, informing managers about their new tasks. Ideally there should be some knowledge and skills training, e.g. in how to conduct a recruitment interview without breaching equal opportunities legislation or the nature and purpose of sickness absence monitoring. Making time for such training may be difficult to justify given the busy lives of most managers, but it may save time later in avoiding employment tribunals or poor performance cases.

EXAMPLE 6.19

One organization took the contrary view that it was best to push their managers in at the deep end; in other words, not to spend much time preparing them for their new responsibilities but to find out the consequences afterwards. Training could then be targeted on real needs, not based on anticipated fears. This was partly to prevent 'difficulty stating' that might otherwise have slowed the change programme.

Education can also be a dynamic process as Example 6.20 shows.

EXAMPLE 6.20

The BBC used 'migration managers' to assist the transition to the new model of HR delivery. These were HR staff assigned to the business division to act as an interface between the project team and line managers. Thus they could explain project details to managers, but also convey their concerns back to the project team. They were in place for some six months from the decision to implement.

Conclusion

How you implement shared services depends a lot on your design and where you are starting from. This chapter can only be a guide to the approach to take. Nevertheless, there is a crucial decision to take around whether or not to pilot aspects of the change and whether or not to phase in a new model, rather than go for a 'big bang'. Training, education and communication are always necessary elements in any change programme. Being clear as to your stakeholders and the part they play in your decision-making will assist in the structuring of your roll-out.

7 Monitoring performance and evaluation

This chapter will look at this often neglected subject, though to be fair many organizations do monitor the performance of their HR services. They look at how customers view the services and how they compare their performance with other organizations. Facilities, like service level agreements, are often used to determine what is expected and provide a template against which performance can be judged. Fewer organizations evaluate the success of their new approach, except perhaps in strictly financial terms. They neither look back to see how much progress has been made nor forward to whether there are better alternatives.

Monitoring performance

The purpose of monitoring in this context can seek to establish the three Es:

- Economy – are shared services saving money?
- Efficiency – are HR processes being streamlined and free from errors?
- Effectiveness – is HR meeting its business objectives?

Monitoring performance can be done in a number of different ways. You can:

- see whether your systems and processes are working as intended – historical focus
- judge how good your performance is – current focus
- test how your customers appreciate your service – internal review
- compare how you are doing against other shared services operations – external review
- monitor to feed into the decision-making process on what to change – future focus.

There are various types of measurement available to you. Some are more useful than others, depending upon your particular requirements:

- Hard measures. These are measures that are easily quantified. Typically included are ratios, percentages and costs. They may be used in a high-level assessment of your performance.
- Process measures. This is a subset of hard measures. These usually look at how well the various processes are operating so they are good at examining operational performance, at least at one level.
- Soft measures. These look at attitudes, perceptions and opinion. These measures can be quantified by applying some sort of measurable scale. They should be used for ascertaining customer views.

One of the advantages of the shared services model is that it allows service provision to be more closely defined. Nevertheless, there is still a tendency to emphasize hard measures simply because they are easily measured and neglect soft measures because the information is more difficult to collect. This may mean that you are not monitoring some of the key aspects of your work. You should use the measures that are appropriate for what you wish to learn and not be constrained by the form of monitoring.

PERFORMANCE CONTRACTS

Some organizations have used their growing capacity to monitor performance to create SLAs between HR and its customers. These 'contracts' usually specify the services offered, their frequency and the quality standards to be expected. They will specify deadlines (on, say, payroll entries), turnaround times (e.g. on processing an offer letter), and targets (e.g. on accuracy of management information). Some companies have gone further and attached a monetary value to the services. This might be through a block charge per SLA (e.g. based on customer head count) or itemized billing for services as used (e.g. per training course). This charging regime needs to be agreed with customers, including the means of distribution of charges if there are multiple organizational users.

There are different views on the benefits of having formal SLAs with a monetary element, compared with informal systems. Proponents of SLAs argue that formalizing the services offered and defining quality standards, make for less ambiguity in expectations. Having a monetary element, it is argued, means that the debate over services is taken seriously. The more commercial orientation of HR may fit a more commercial attitude in the business more generally. HR is then using terms and techniques familiar to their line customers and ones that give credibility to the HR offering. Charges can be market tested. This keeps HR on its toes and reassures customers that they are being given a competitive price for their work. Clients are more particular in what they seek; suppliers know that the services offered are needed. It also gives staff real targets at which to aim. Financially based SLAs are also more likely to put a brake on what one service provider described as 'creeping service development'. In other words, there is a tendency for customers to add service requests without acknowledging the resource implications. Defining precisely what is being offered in terms the customer can understand, and equally what is not on offer, and then pricing it may prevent customers getting extra for free.

The contrary argument is that the monitoring process generates such activity that the point of the exercise, the substantive content of the work, takes second place to the process of measuring it. Some organizations are put off by the investment in financial systems necessary for proper service costing. The former seems a stronger argument than the latter. Part of the benefit of shared services is that it allows you to provide better management information. This is because it can be collated at a single point and using a single information platform. You then really need to understand the financial implications of the services that can come from using something like *activity-based costing*. However, monitoring can become an industry in itself if one is not too careful. So care needs to be taken in setting up an SLA to get the level of detail right – sufficient to track but not overly burdensome.

Whether you choose to have formal or informal SLAs or not, there is a strong argument for having some clearly defined and public metrics. This is because of the very nature and sensitivity of many of the shared services' outputs, e.g. payroll or pension payments. It is good practice to have robust measures to counter the potential for false perceptions, often gleaned by one or two high-profile errors, of a poor service. Whilst perceptions cannot be so easily overcome, it does help focus on relative scale of service delivery problems rather than rely on an anecdotal approach.

PERFORMANCE ASSESSMENT

This is the most common type of measurement. Many SLAs concentrate on process performance – how quickly and accurately a variety of tasks are performed. Here monitoring is about meeting standards of service provision to ensure that output is to the requisite level in terms of timeliness or accuracy. This can in part be achieved by putting in place quality control measures that lay down standard procedures, supported by performance metrics. This enables you to determine how quickly, for example, an offer letter, processed after an interview or a promotion, can be generated. Results can then be tracked. For more complicated processes, such as supporting a maternity case, systems can flag when action is required, thereby reducing the chances of error by omission.

For call centre systems you can track call volumes looking at the peaks and troughs of when calls are made. This allows you to adjust resourcing levels to match workload. Performance can be assessed via waiting times, call duration and content. Again this may help with staffing, but more likely it will be valuable to determine training needs. The latter will be centred on the call centre staff to cover gaps in their knowledge, but, as Compaq does (IDS, 2001), you can also use it to see where the calls are coming from and the nature of the questions. This can then lead to training initiatives in the customer areas that seem ignorant of company policies and procedures.

Similarly, monitoring can be used to check that people know their area of expertise, and do not go beyond their capability. This can be managed through having the sort of *escalation* procedures described in Chapter 3.

You can extend monitoring to 'cases', i.e. problems under investigation. Information gathered through phone calls or face-to-face discussion can be logged, along with actions taken. This gives a record of the case for the files, essential if ever there were to be disciplinary or legal consequences. It also allows you to see patterns, e.g. an increase in bullying cases, or a rise in disputes within a particular department.

Measuring performance can include fault-finding as another aspect of system control. More than in the past, errors are likely to be visible and not easily suppressed.

CUSTOMER OPINION

Besides monitoring performance metrics internally, you can undertake customer satisfaction checks. This might be specific reaction to a service delivered (e.g. a training course) at point of use. Are they satisfied with the service? Intranets may have an email return facility to generate feedback on the content and layout of intranet pages. Alternatively, you can include specific pages on the intranet to allow comments to be made. Broader responses may be required to get an overall picture of the view of the HR offering. Questionnaires (paper based or on-line) are probably the best means to establish customer views on quality, timeliness and cost of the service. Random phone calls can also be used to probe in more depth.

EXAMPLE 7.1

IBM measures its levels of customer satisfaction with its service centre. In 1999 the user approval level was running at about 90 per cent.

Some organizations have customer panels to agree service provision and monitor outcomes. The advantage here is that you get a more sophisticated and informed response. The danger is that the panellists cease to be typical customers.

EXAMPLE 7.2

The East Dorset Management and Support Services Agency offers a broad-based shared services approach to a number of local NHS Trusts. It has a 'stakeholder' group that reflects its customers and the internal management function. It is chaired by a non-executive director of the parent Trust and its purpose is to oversee the activities of the Agency and to agree future developments. The committee also agrees the pricing structure – both levels and means.

Another approach is to use your business-facing HR managers to gather customer views and report back to the shared services operation. This means you do not get direct feedback, but it might mean that the HR managers can help create realistic expectations of the services delivered.

EXAMPLE 7.3

Powergen uses an annual survey of business unit HR departments. This means that those who pay for services judge them. This is accepted as an indirect assessment for employees and line managers. There is a risk that HR only hears complaints and thus gets a distorted view of the shared service centre's performance. This is mitigated by the fact that in the headquarters the service centre staff tend to get to know their customers because they are in the same building. This is not easy for the sites.

Each service is appraised on:

- quality
- timeliness
- satisfaction.

Criticism is followed up. This may mean taking action to improve matters or challenging the basis of the criticism, which may in turn require explaining the realities of life in terms of, say, cost or corporate policy.

BENCHMARKING

Another useful part of monitoring you can attempt is benchmarking your service provision against external markers. This can be especially useful when comparing delivery costs with those of other organizations. The trick, though, is to find comparable organizations, whose circumstances are sufficiently similar to your own and where you can trust the data. Indeed, the experience already of some shared services benchmarking groups is that organizations' processes are so vastly different that it does not make for very realistic comparisons between them. That said, like the HR:employee ratio, referred to on page 49, whilst imperfect, it does give an indication of where one stands by comparison with others. The new outsourcing players may be making this task better through articulating an administrative cost per employee benchmark (currently £400) and this may be a useful target against which to measure the success or otherwise of a cost-driven shared services strategy.

CONCLUSION

These means of monitoring can be combined to provide a holistic view of performance that can be a real help when looking to see what further improvements can be made, as Example 7.4 testifies.

EXAMPLE 7.4

Metrics are used at Ford to assess performance in seven key areas:

- system response times
- user likes and dislikes
- feature and functionality awareness
- ease of use and overall usability
- barriers to usage
- effectiveness of communication efforts
- what is missing? (Ashton, 2001)

In the context of shared services, Table 7.1 offers some suggestions of what you might monitor and why.

Table 7.1 Examples of measures to be monitored

Internal efficiency:

- time taken between vacancy lodged on internal job advertising system and job offer made
- cost of recruitment per recruit
- proportion of induction packs issued on time
- percentage of payroll entry errors against target of zero
- relocation costs within budget
- number of training courses delivered
- speed of response to telephone calls at the call centre

Internal effectiveness:

- value rating for trainees on internal courses
- customer satisfaction rate for users of call centre

- competence level of line managers in performance management skills
- proportion of jobs with descriptions and evaluation scores
- salaries match market median

Outcome measures:

- reduced levels of sickness absence
- appropriate voluntary resignation rate
- improved employee morale and commitment
- payroll cost per unit of output
- proportion of ethnic minorities in management roles
- number of days lost through industrial action
- number of employment tribunal cases
- proportion of staff rated fully competent to do their jobs

Care needs to be exercised to ensure that the right amount of monitoring is done. You can get information overload where more data is produced than can reasonably be processed. There is a fine line between using performance statistics to guide your training, resourcing and quality review, and generating too much paperwork for busy people.

Evaluation

Shared services systems can access a wealth of information that can be monitored. This can be helpful but be of limited value unless you learn from the results, especially where there have been problems. Too many projects have been implemented without proper review. Whilst regular monitoring picks up service deficiencies in timeliness, quality or cost, some service failures may not be registered. What if potential users are bypassing HR services? For example, a line manager dissatisfied with recruitment through HR goes out and hires his/her own staff. Or a manager frustrated by the administrative service from HR sets up his/her own parallel operation.

At one level, evaluating the performance of your shared services operation is integral to monitoring. You can judge how well your service is working through customer opinion surveys, from how well strategic objectives are being met, by how many system breakdowns there are, etc. But a true evaluation would go beyond service-level information. You should be able to sit back from this continual checking and ask more fundamental questions. These might include:

- How well are your business objectives being served by this particular configuration of HR?
- Are there spin-offs in terms of organizational performance (e.g. improved productivity) or organizational health (e.g. more positive employee attitudes)?
- Could an alternative structure serve the organization better?
- Are you correctly distributing your activities between line managers and HR, and within HR, between shared services, the corporate centre and business-facing HR managers?
- Is the right balance (in terms of business priorities) being achieved in terms of cost-effectiveness and innovation to meet customer needs?
- Are all your customers being properly served or are there biases against some?
- Is your communication as effective as it might be in terms of keeping customers informed and getting feedback?

- Are you right to continue with the current distribution of activities between in house and outsourcing?
- Is your technology working as effectively as it might?

In conducting such a review you would use your monitoring data but look at it with more of a critical, long-term eye. Thus customer satisfaction survey information should be broken down by customer type and service area to find any weak areas. If some are uncovered you might want to investigate in more depth, say by conducting focus groups to discuss problems in more detail. Similarly, your benchmarking information would need to look at service standards and costs for each activity. If any areas seem to be expensive, you might seek an external quote. So, for example, if, by comparison with comparable organizations, your training delivery looks to be pricey, then you could examine whether a contractor could do the job more cheaply. Matters are not so straightforward if delivery standards are not up to the quality experienced elsewhere. You are better to spend time understanding the causes rather than rushing out to choose an alternative supplier. This might be the conclusion of the review that you need external expertise to lift standards, but, as we remarked earlier, it is bad practice to export unresolved problems.

Technological difficulties should be self-evident. It should be obvious if there are service failures with a new payroll or HRIS. A non-functioning call centre or intranet is also likely to be obvious. Again monitoring the performance of technology will lead you to discover evident failures, but you need to go further in an evaluation. Are problems persisting because you have the wrong kit? Is it the connectivity between the various devices that does not work as it should? Are you asking your systems to deliver that which it is impossible for them to deliver? How much is it the technology that is failing and how much those who are operating it? Especially with obtaining management information, the deficiencies are more often that garbage is put in and that is what you get out.

A more challenging aspect of evaluation is to see whether you are getting the right balance between cost control and innovation. This means, are you maximizing opportunities to exploit economies of scale by bringing service delivery outlets together wherever possible, by offering standardized products and by using the cheapest means to interact with your customers? Is this in line with what the business requires of you? Conversely, are you meeting your customer needs in terms of the products you offer and the way they are delivered? Most organizations would probably want to strike an appropriate balance between cost control and delighting the customer. Where and how you draw this line is a matter of judgement.

Then there is the question of structure to consider. Is your shared services operation working well? Have you got the right components within it, both in terms of delivery mechanisms (call centre, intranet, etc.) and the services delivered from it (recruitment, training administration, etc.)? Is the balance right between what you have in your corporate office and what you have in shared services? For example, could you usefully transfer, say, succession planning to the shared services operation from the corporate HR team? Or is the balance wrong the other way round? Does the governance function need strengthening to bring greater consistency to the way people are managed across the business? Other structural changes you might consider are creating centres of excellence in your policy group, reconfiguring the way the consultancy team is set up or shifting some administrative functions out of/into the shared services from the activities they support, e.g. training or recruitment.

Then there is the relationship between HR and the line to review. Assuming you have business-facing HR managers, are they successfully providing a strategic contribution to the businesses they support? If not, is this because of the skills they lack or insufficient ambition in customer aspirations? Do the line manager customers value this role? Are the reporting relationships to business and HR leaders working well? Besides the direct HR involvement, how effectively are employees being managed by their managers? Are the managers sufficiently skilled and resourced to do this job? Are they getting the right support from HR? In other words, is devolvement working? Should it be pushed further and more activities transferred from the shared services operation to managers to undertake themselves? Alternatively, are managers already overwhelmed by what they are being asked to do? Can HR shared services help to relieve that burden?

A more fundamental question is whether shared services is delivering the cost, productivity and service benefits you expected? This should relate to the reasons why you introduced shared services in the first place. If your strategy was to lift the level of HR contribution and the evidence is that HR is still a short-term fire-fighting function, then remedial action will be required. If you wanted to drive down the expense of people management activities, you might see the cost of the HR function falling but the spend diverted to business unit managers. This, too, would cause you to investigate further. If quality uplift is the goal, then you would want to see standards rise. Most organizations would not be so one-eye focused that they would fix on only one goal at the expense of everything else. The drive for quality enhancement cannot come at any price. The need for cost reduction should not result in service quality plummeting.

In any scenario you are likely to check how well the productivity of your HR team is developing. This is likely to be more true for your administrative activities than transformational activities. You can review how well the performance metrics are being met. The higher value-added tasks may be more difficult to measure, but you can go beyond simply looking at, say, the number of consulting days per head to trying to evaluate the impact of the interventions. Has the organization moved forward as a result of the advice given, the process designed or the policy evaluated?

Your evaluation should aim to identify any unwelcome problems (such as those listed in Chapter 9) and especially those that are so difficult to solve that an alternative approach (e.g. of service delivery segmented by business unit) might be better. This is a tough question to answer, but if your shared services approach is not working in terms of cost or quality, you are better off discovering this and facing up to the consequences.

EXAMPLE 7.5

Cable and Wireless has developed a four level evaluation as follows:

Level One: Reaction

- Line satisfaction audit pre-implementation
- e-HR communications audit
- SAP training 'happy sheets'.

Level Two: Learning

- SAP training knowledge check
- Online follow-up survey.

Level Three: Transfer

- Helpdesk query analysis
- 360-degree feedback
- Performance appraisal.

Level Four: Business Results

- Line satisfaction audit post-implementation
- Business measurements
- Interviews/focus groups.

This combines a number of aspects of evaluation, including customer satisfaction, customer understanding and business benefits, in an integrated manner.

Evaluation does not have to be static or only to be conducted at the end of an exercise as Example 7.6 shows.

EXAMPLE 7.6

The BBC used a form of evaluate as you go. Since their implementation was staged they could use the learning from introducing shared services for one business cluster to the next. This was done through putting up the issues or problems that arose on flipcharts placed in the HR Operations work area. The list was reviewed at the end of each day. Things that could be decided there and then were settled; other matters were taken away for later consideration. All the ideas and solutions were incorporated, where appropriate, in the roll out of the next stage of implementation.

So far, this book has considered a number of different issues involved in creating HR shared services and has illustrated these points through the use of short examples to explain how some organizations have tackled these problems.

However, to bring the points to greater life, a case study has been written by an HR shared services practitioner that documents from real-life experience how the Royal Bank of Scotland Group faced up to the challenge of getting best value from HR.

As we have seen in the first seven chapters of this book, HR shared services is rarely the only part of realigning HR, but it is often the catalyst. Progress within RBS is described in Chapter 8 where the starting point is not the luxury of a blank piece of paper, but one where a number of different challenges have to be faced during implementation, not least the acquisition of a company three times larger than itself.

The case study gives a synopsis of progress over a three-and-a-half-year period but the specific learnings are included in Chapter 9 along with the many others described in this book.

8 Case study: the Royal Bank of Scotland Group

At the beginning of this book, we described how HR functions have been having a turbulent time recently, some of it self-created to strive to find a value-added role in organizations and some as a result of more drastic cost-cutting issues.

In keeping with many of the drivers for shared services described in this book, the RBS case study summarizes some of the ways in which it is trying to avoid being seen as an 'expense', but one which adds value to the business. Hopefully, this chapter not only describes what the often used but rarely defined 'value-added' means, but how important the role of the HR shared services is in that transformation.

Today, the Royal Bank of Scotland Group (RBSG) is one of the largest organizations in the UK, employing around 100 000 staff globally and, based on market capitalization, one of the top-three banks in Europe and number five in the world. This scale has arisen through innovative growth and the successful acquisition of the NatWest Group in early 2000. Included in the RBSG stable are well-known brands such as Direct Line, Tesco Personal Finance, Virgin One, Coutts, Lombard, Ulster Bank and, within the USA, the enlarged Citizens Financial Group. Of course, the well-known UK high street names of RBS and NatWest remain.

The case study is based on the progression of the RBS HR function (pre- and post-acquisition of NatWest) over a four-year period and charts the key steps in the move from a highly fragmented, but respected personnel function supporting 22 000 employees, to an HR function dealing with 100 000 employees across a more diverse range of businesses and geographies. It is a study of a journey with much still to achieve.

Historical context

For the case study to be more easily readable, the historical context of the HR function within the NatWest Group has been ignored until the point of acquisition in early 2000. Whilst there are many similarities the prevailing structure and culture within NatWest before this date does not facilitate such a clear understanding and emerging picture as the RBS story will hopefully do. This does not diminish the enormity of the implications on the RBS HR function in dealing with the acquired function, and we will look at this in more depth in section 5 of this chapter.

As with any traditional organization (the RBS story started in 1727) the case study does not start with a blank sheet of paper on which theory is implemented perfectly. The starting point for this reflection takes an appropriate start date of January 1998, timed just after the then recent arrival of a new HR Director with an agenda for change.

The base point for the case study is an HR function with well-respected senior personnel professionals positioned within the Service and Operations Departments division within the

Royal Bank Group but supporting, in addition to this mainly back-office sector, the two principal income generating businesses, Retail Financial Services and Corporate and Institutional Banking (CIB). Also, within the Group were two completely separate business sectors: Direct Line Group, providing a range of general insurance products to an increasing market within the UK; and Citizens Financial Group, a developing retail franchise centred around the north-east of the USA. Both had (and to this day have) their own devolved HR functions.

The principal issues with the HR function in early 1998 can be summarized into a few key points:

- respected personnel professionals providing a robust service in more traditional areas of training, employee relations and employment law, compensation, recruitment and general HR advice
- positioned at the wrong level of the organization's decision-making processes and considered more as a 'support' function with a limited remit at the senior management level on more strategic HR issues
- local delivery was provided through a number of fragmented teams split across the three market sectors, Service and Operations, Retail and CIB, but all with a direct report line through the HR Director into the Service and Operations division
- each team provided a full service provision ranging from local keying of all HR input to an in house HR system to advice to senior management on a range of people issues
- only payroll and pensions administration were centralized but with separated reporting lines and little alignment
- no clear articulated HR strategy but with a developing vision of moving the prevailing business perception from a low-value operational (but critical) function to one which can help the business grow through proactively driving the people agenda
- no clear HR delivery strategy but with a desire to improve the customer service element and seek efficiencies of operation.

Two key early steps for the HR Director, Neil Roden, were to appoint a new HR Leadership team with a shared agenda for change and to reposition the whole function within an emerging business structure; the creation of a UK bank to bring together the Retail, CIB and Service and Operations divisions into a more aligned business. The creation of the UK bank also meant that the HR function stepped up and out of the 'support' division and into the UK bank centre. At the highest level, it was the first representation at the most senior management level of decision-making (accepting that the Group now comprised three pretty autonomous businesses and the UK bank was by far the largest).

Whilst the repositioning was positive, the agenda for change within HR was now more readily apparent, albeit somewhat short on detail. Key issues present at the time were:

- no real cohesive understanding of the customer proposition (and a significant variance in perceptions at senior levels about what HR was there to do)
- the recent appointments of new functional heads into HR Services and HR Information with an undeveloped mandate to build a more cohesive shared services and information management infrastructure
- varying degrees of acceptance for the need for change within HR by the senior management with a sense of potential loss coming from the likely implications of any programme of change

- a very hierarchical HR structure (with over a dozen different levels) and top-down culture but with a director-led desire to flatten.

With this background, the need for a change programme was becoming increasingly apparent and project Chrysalis was born. At this point, and with the benefit of hindsight, the case study is summarized into five key stages:

1 Building the change programme.
2 Current state assessment.
3 High-level design.
4 Implementation.
5 Recent events.

The principal conclusions from the RBS experience of the key pitfalls to avoid, have been incorporated into Chapter 9.

1   Building the change programme

The establishment of the change programme in 1999 was in itself used to start to address some of the key issues by some of the ways in which the project was positioned. There were three main facets to this stage of the journey:

- building commitment for change across the stakeholders
- creating the right methodology and high-level approach
- selecting the key project resources.

COMMITMENT TO CHANGE

The key stakeholders at the time fell into three camps: the strategic business unit (SBU) leaders (between 50 and 75 senior managers), the senior HR team and the HR employees in general. The HR community was segmented because of the different implications to the senior HR team and to HR employees generally. For the customer groupings, only the SBU leaders were consulted as opposed to employees because of the focus of the change required, i.e. strategic repositioning of the HR proposition.

Taking each in turn, the SBU leaders were canvassed on two general topics: what do you think of the HR function today and what do you want from it in future? Whilst this is also covered in the current-state assessment below, in terms of commitment to change, this was not a process on which the HR executive wished to dwell. This was not meant as an arrogant 'we know best' but more that the organizational climate did not encourage such a 'blank sheet' approach. In terms of commitment it was perceived that HR needed to develop a credible proposition first and then seek feedback. With such an array of views about what HR was there to do, this seemed a logical approach to take.

For the senior HR team, the programme presented either an opportunity or a threat. It would be a simplification to say that those new to the organization relished the opportunity, whilst those who had been present for a while were threatened by the prospect. That said, the approach taken was direct and to an extent mandatory. Buy-in to the move from a more operational and traditional personnel function to a value-adding HR function was assumed, regardless of potential personal losses.

For the HR employees in general, the changes also posed threats and opportunities, depending on their role. For business-aligned resources, it signalled a chance to move away from transactional discussions with line (payroll queries, form filling, holiday entitlements, and so on) to more value-added roles looking at maximizing performance of staff, supporting change programmes, developing programmes to retain and motivate staff, and offering a proposition to the market for talent which rivals competitors. For administrative resources, the implied threat was a move away from that activity and with it the commensurate concerns about job security.

At this stage, acknowledgement of the different positions was made but with an explicit overall message for change still reinforced.

CREATING THE RIGHT APPROACH

Given the overall context at the time and indeed some of the cultural issues, getting the right approach to the change programme was key. In essence there were probably three options:

- desktop review by remote project team and creation of future state ratified by HR leadership
- bottom-up detailed analysis of current state and strategy for future through presentation and support by HR leadership
- top-down assessment of current state and articulation of future by HR leadership.

The prevailing culture at the time suggested the latter approach would be most appropriate as it allowed control to remain with the senior management. How accurate an assessment of the real position and how stretching the solutions would be as a result remain to this day unknown.

Thus, to start to use the actual programme to change cultural issues as well as build a case for change, the middle option was chosen. Indeed, it would not only deliver a more accurate and detailed current-state position, but it would challenge one of the other targets for the change programme, the hierarchy.

The current-state assessment section (page 118) will describe with more granularity the approach taken. However, in terms of building the change agenda, involving employees at every level would challenge the thinking and start to convey how we wanted the function to work in future real time.

GETTING THE RIGHT RESOURCES

At a high level, the resources for the programme fell into three categories:

- change agents
- technical resources
- stakeholders.

Again the resources used with the bottom-up approach can start to change the current state through process. The key facets of the programme were:

- Appointment of a team champion from each area of HR, who could not be the most senior member of that team – this challenged the hierarchy, provided a learning opportunity for individuals not used to such challenges and ensured an uncensored level of honesty.
- Sign-off procedures for the senior HR managers in each team – this did not allow material change of the bottom-up analysis without overt notification to the core team but did allow local ownership of the analysis.
- Two steering groups, in terms of content and direction – the collective senior HR managers were the first point of escalation. Second, the HR leadership was engaged as the ultimate decision-making body for structural and strategic changes.
- A small core team led by the recently appointed Head of HR Services as Project Director who brought no preconceived thinking about the current state and who had laid out a vision of creating a shared services function, supported at least in conceptual terms by the HR leadership.
- External support from KPMG to provide the technical infrastructure for the activity review but, more importantly for the project director, a sounding board and shield for and from the rest of the HR function.

This mix of internal and external, senior and junior, generalist and specialist HR resources meant that the programme should at least be balanced. It also meant that the current cultural status quo was being challenged from the start.

2   Current-state assessment

The base case assessment, frequently known in consulting circles as the 'as is' could be categorized into five key tenets:

- customer
- cost
- quality
- capability
- technology.

(In this case study, customers are the employees of the Group, including line managers and business leaders.)

Project Chrysalis looked at all five categories to differing degrees but with strong emphasis on current cost/quality and, to a much lesser degree, the needs of its customer for the reasons described earlier in this chapter under building commitment for change. Each of the categories is described in detail.

CUSTOMER

The case study has already documented the rationale for a base assessment of customers' views of the current position and stated needs from HR going forward. However, this review was tempered by a belief that the organization needed a more concrete 'straw man' proposition before seeking formal commitment to the changes desired by HR itself.

The views were collated using a very straightforward questionnaire and a simple score from one to five of the current capability of the function and qualitative comments on what was required for the future. In terms of the current state, the view was that the function was competent in most areas (averaging 3.7) but needed to focus on two key issues going forward. First, get the basics right and, second, add more value. Whilst the former is pretty obvious, the latter is always perceived differently multiplied by how many different views are sought. What the survey did do, though, was to prove that any model that created a more robust operational delivery capability and freed up business-facing resources to add more value would be hitting the broadest of targets.

COST

The focus of Project Chrysalis to many was to get a better understanding of the current-state activity analysis with a particular focus on costs and cost drivers. It was perceived that any change incentive would have to come from an agenda which highlighted how centralization into a shared services function of HR processing (whatever that meant) would reduce costs through scale efficiencies.

Other than the roles and use of a change management approach in the team selection and approach documented earlier, the core activity analysis used is a very common methodology. The work of the HR function was broken down into 18 activities each consisting of between four and seven tasks against which over 200 HR staff completed a four-week study of their activities. The work was annualized to account for seasonal variations and tested against peer groups for anomalies. The aforementioned steering group signed off the activity 'dictionary' and each project champion and team manager signed off the analysis as a true picture, ensuring discussion focused on the action arising from the outputs not to question the validity of the data per se.

In terms of results, estimated costs were split as follows:

- Over 60 per cent of activity was deemed administrative.
- *Circa* 25 per cent was deemed advisory.
- *Circa* 15 per cent or less was deemed 'value added' or strategic business partnering.

This used the well-known, to many HR professionals, 'Ulrich model' as a guide. Two facts emerging in particular summed up the level of work in which the function was engaged:

- The HR function spent more time collecting appraisal forms for filing than reviewing the overall performance trends arising from the ratings.
- About a fifth of all HR activity was recruitment related, albeit less than 1 per cent was spent on understanding the broader business-resourcing picture.

Whilst the activity and cost data was useful, the need to get underneath cost drivers proved more elusive. The simple purpose was to have a clearer understanding of what activity changes could be made including centralization and which could be stopped altogether, which should be increased and which should be left locally (such as recruitment interviews). Unfortunately, the other implication of such a devolved HR base at the time was that there was no consistent metric capture on volumes, quality or turnaround times (clearly all activities were produced much quicker than by a subsequently centralized team, despite no metrics at the time!). Thus, for the base case, core productivity could not be identified and, more importantly, comparisons to the subsequent shared services function were also not possible.

Once the data had been gathered, the subsequent focus on process inefficiencies and opportunities was enough to identify the key change projects that would increase the value HR could add. A target reduction of 25 per cent of administrative activity to be replaced by more strategic changes (documented elsewhere) was made; a key plank of this strategy would be the creation of a true shared services function with appropriate metrics, process maps and service level agreements. These aspects are covered in the Quality section below.

QUALITY

One of the most potentially valuable aspects of a current-state assessment is to ascertain the current quality of processes such as time to recruit new employees or even time to produce a new hire contract within that process. Not only does the assessment present opportunities for future improvement it also enables comparisons externally through specialist benchmark organizations such as EP-First (Saratoga). In the RBS exercise, unfortunately, the small amount of local data collation within the devolved HR structure at the time made quality assessments difficult. The real issue is that this has negated meaningful comparisons with the shared service function that arose from the activity analysis and, thus, perceptions of a reduced level of service cannot be verified or disproved.

As this case study develops, the reader will understand that whilst shared services does facilitate the importance and clear accountability of service quality, the lack of a base point back in 1999 remains a significant issue in 2002 when proving or otherwise the case for shared services.

CAPABILITY

The overall change programme involved a switch from administrative and personnel advisory activity to more strategic added-value work. However, this raised two vital questions:

- What is strategic added-value work?
- What resources and skills are required to deliver that work?

Whilst this book is focused on the creation of shared services, the wider HR changes that it facilitates are very relevant. Indeed, the review of current skills gave great insight into what the total RBS HR skill-set was.

To answer the first question, a short piece of consultative work was instigated looking at the day-to-day work of key HR resources (using external consultancy objectively to assess this against a structured competency set). Out of this review, both key work attributes (e.g. openness to change, relationship-building skills, good diagnostic awareness) and good examples of strategic work (e.g. facilitating business change programmes, coaching to SBU leaders, etc.) became evident. Whilst good examples of strategic HR were not widely prevalent, it gave a good basis for what RBS HR was trying to move towards.

This work was then developed using an external occupational psychology consultancy to create six core RBS HR 'consulting' competencies and a development centre against which all (except about 30 pure payroll/pensions administrators) the RBS HR resources would be tested. At the macro level, this gave a RBS HR skill-set analysis; at the micro level, it gave about 200 employees a good appreciation of where they fitted against the new consulting model. The six core competencies were:

- diagnostic and advisory skills
- managerial skills
- communication and influencing skills
- enhancing professionalism
- value delivery focus
- change and implementation skills.

The macro level analysis demonstrated that RBS HR was well equipped for professional HR advice but did not have the capability to deliver a total consultancy service with less than 10 per cent of resources identified as being capable at 'business partner' level today. It also demonstrated that the bottom 25–30 per cent of resources was not deemed to be able to make the switch to consultancy working even at the analyst/associate level. This latter group, however, could have the right skills for delivering the shared services function, not because the skills are substandard (although there could be cultural perception by those who did score highly in the development centre that this was the case), but because the skill-set is completely different where attention to detail, supervisor skills, work flow and operations management are much more relevant.

TECHNOLOGY

The final area of assessment and increasingly important in human resources is the area of HRIS.

This section will not prescribe the right HRIS strategy for the reader as many different factors have to be considered. Key factors include:

- size of organization
- scope of organization
- business structure
- geographical boundaries
- legislative differences (especially data protection)
- organizational technology capabilities – i.e. make or buy
- business priorities and availability of financial resources
- nature of the business (better examples of good HRIS come from those organizations whose core business it is)
- organizational culture (centralized or devolved).

For RBS, the recognition of moving to a more widely supported HRIS in PeopleSoft was taken before the shared services concept was formulated and this provided a good platform from which to move, being both scalable and, with iteration, robust for future requirements. The new platform would mean changes for many users, but the future needs of the function, not least the creation of the RBSelect flexible benefits scheme launched in 1998, required a new HRIS infrastructure.

To conclude the current-state assessment, the general synopsis was that RBS HR had a set of varying customer needs but with two clear messages: get the core HR right and seek to add more value. It had identified cost drivers and ways of removing waste, however it also identified areas where information on service quality was deficient, an issue that would 'bite back' in later stages. RBS HR had a good idea of its resource stock and the recruitment and development priorities. Finally, it had a basis for a robust technology platform from which to deliver sound HR processes and the increasing appetite for information as a diagnostic tool for consultancy work.

3   High-level design

Having created the 'as is' basis for change, good consultants will now advise that the 'to be' has to be determined. This section documents how RBS HR designed its 'to be' across six key areas:

- structure
- make or buy
- customer fit
- processes
- roles and accountabilities
- monitoring and reporting.

STRUCTURE

The overall model for shared services (the latest version of which is shown in Figure 8.1) had been established with the appointment of the Head of HR Services in summer 1998, albeit with an initial remit of pensions and payroll as the centre of shared services. The standing

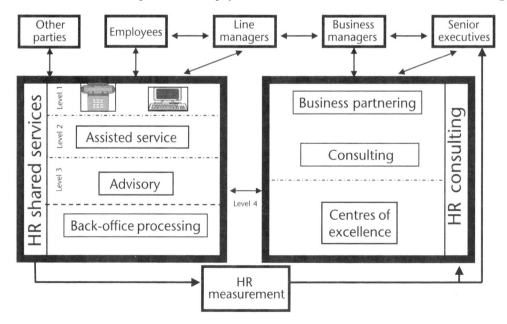

Figure 8.1   RBS delivery model, 2002

assumption from the current-state assessment was that further centralization into a shared services function would follow with the amalgamation of all HR processing into a new HR Service Centre, an assumption which was ratified. The intention of aligning HR processing (e.g. keying new hires into PeopleSoft) with payroll (the end of many processes and often where visibility of process failures are most prevalent) should also have commensurate effects on process quality.

At the time, both Citizens (US based) and Direct Line were considered out of scope but all UK operations were included. The offshore (Channel Islands) HR processing was also kept out of scope. These decisions were about clearing up 'low-hanging fruit' rather than creating anything more substantial. It was also key to establishing the model and service before widening both the brief but also the complexity.

At the time, the decision to centralize the HR processing into the centre was made through the influence of the current-state analysis rather than reliance on any organizational business model, although this was to change following the NatWest acquisition some two years later. This latter aspect is covered in section 5 in this chapter which describes more recent events.

MAKE OR BUY

Having established that the shared services remit would be payroll, pensions administration and HR processing, how this would be delivered was then discussed. At this point, the flexible benefits scheme had been outsourced (as there was no internal capability and little UK knowledge of how to run these schemes at the time) to Hewitt Associates, a US domiciled but increasingly global HR/benefits consultancy and administration function. This included a well-liked telephony front end using trained customer service representatives (rather than script readers) who used technology to interpret rather than recite by rote. Many organizations do not have such an option when considering make or buy, RBS did.

Thus, having established broad support for the creation of a shared services function across the key stakeholders in the Group, the opportunity to deliver a customer-friendly 'front end' to HR processes, payroll and pensions was considered. The latter two needed too much technical knowledge at this point and were discounted. However the opportunity to take advantage of the scale and capability of the outsourced call centre was taken for some key HR processes. The selection of the processes to be outsourced was based on three key questions:

- Can Hewitt do this better using their customer focus and technology?
- Will the process be enhanced by case management?
- Can Hewitt deliver this process from the technology feeds from PeopleSoft?

If the answers to these questions were yes, this HR process was outsourced. Thus, maternity processing (including timely outbound calls), referencing (financial and employment), HR policy and procedural information provision and key management information (MI) reports (described below) were outsourced. This latter service has proved somewhat innovative in that all leavers, joiners and people who turn down joining RBS are given a structured questionnaire to complete to enable RBS HR to have a richer base of information from which to build attractive and motivational employment propositions. Whilst not fully embedded and utilized 18 months after launch, the basis that this service offers is at the core of the HR consultant proposition to the business, i.e. using good quality information to shape the people agenda in the business.

Whilst influence through the current-state analysis proved useful, the use of outsourcing can also be used as a catalyst for change and that was true for RBS too. Using an external organization's skills, reputation, technology and people can often prove fruitful in convincing those more sceptical in an organization of the potential value of centralization over and above pure cost savings. It was true for RBS that the move from local processing to central shared services, even outsourced, was perceived by some customer groups as a deterioration in service (even though measures to prove or otherwise this view were not available in the previous model). By using better technology, external customer focus and technical experts in their field, this should help change the perceptions.

The other use of an external supplier for RBS was more latterly during the integration of NatWest where scale and volatility in demand for key HR services can be better met through a combination of internal and external support. Again, this is covered in section 5 of this chapter more fully.

Even some two years after the first outsourcing, it is still too early to state clearly whether this has been a success or not; that too will be considered later.

CUSTOMER FIT

It has already been intimated that certain segments of customers perceived the move from local to central would result in a deterioration of service. Notwithstanding the absence of robust measures to support or refute this, the model established was to try to accommodate local fit into the centralization strategy. Using the tests established in this book, it would fit with the shared services ethos where the customer is king rather than pure centralization where cost savings tend to be the primary goal. Thus for example, the three Retail Network bank areas did have some say in how processes could be applied to meet its different groups needs even though this has created issues when the scale of the organization grew. Additional steps in processes to distribute induction materials and check on probation period completion were added for Retail customers in the interests of business buy-in to the shared services concept.

On a more macro level, the ethos of the bank in its own provision of services can be summed up as 'on the street, on the PC, on the phone'. The customer delivery model of RBS HR mirrors this to a large degree giving choice at the bottom end of services (such as information provision, address changes, etc.) to the cheaper transactional tools of intranet, IVR and telephony generally. The more value-added HR advisory work has historically been delivered face to face, although this too had started to change to telephony at the end of 2001 through the creation of an HR Advisory Centre.

PROCESSES

Having established the overarching structure and remit (whether the service is delivered internally or externally and indeed whether the model fits with customer expectations), it is key to document the processes involved. Whilst considered an obvious statement to make, in RBS's experience, this step was not considered enough (see the conclusions in Chapter 9) and, as a prerequisite to agreeing roles and responsibilities, especially where processes are fragmented as is often the case in HR, was a critical lesson.

During the current-state assessment, the work included process charts documenting key process failures, potential opportunities for improvement and an overall assessment of the cost per process. For example, the recruitment process included seven different segments (e.g. attraction, selection, induction) and a number of activities within each segment (e.g. role profile creation, newspaper advert, shortlisting, etc.). Across the process map at least 10 different parties were identified (e.g. line manager, candidate, HR) and thus the scope for failures were numerous (41 were identified). Known as 'brown paper' exercises in consulting circles, these maps were presented to the HR leadership in establishing where processes were broken and what options there were to improve. Suggested 'to be' process maps captured these ideas.

In this design stage, these new process maps were used as the basis for business facing HR teams to challenge, change and embed these into the shared services function and to 'sell' to a sceptical customer base. As will be demonstrated in Chapter 9, whilst this initial push got the buy-in needed, regular reminders and better communication direct to line managers on the processes were necessities missed.

ROLES AND ACCOUNTABILITIES

It does follow that having agreed the scope of the share services function, the balance between customer wants and central efficiencies, the 'as is' and 'to be' processes documented, roles and accountabilities need to be laid out. These are not just the sole preserve of the shared services function, although many in the industry will know it often feels that way!

The Royal Bank of Scotland involved a number of business-facing and functional technical experts in the process design described above. This is not just good practice for change management, it actually allows the people who do the job the chance to shape what would work best for their customers. On the flip side, this 'consultative' approach does lead to a longer lead time for design and perhaps too much customization where none is genuinely needed. RBS did follow this approach and created many materials, including process maps, with key roles identified. It was agreed at the time that the best way of managing a customer who expects a detraction in service levels was to 'hand hold' by the local HR team remaining at the instigation of processes with the service centre rather than the line direct. On reflection this was a mistake but again this point is reinforced in Chapter 9.

Whilst the processes did have more local HR involved than was really necessary, even though it was for good reasons, it did create too many process hand-offs between different groups. For example, a contract request form would be completed by the line to the local HR and then sent to the service centre even though the line could have sent this direct. Over time, as people changed at the local HR level, the loss of knowledge and understanding of roles in that process chain have deteriorated with a commensurate loss of service. This gives rise to two thoughts:

- Even if the customer is not sure about shared services, go for the full process change and do not make allowances for perceived customer benefits; non-standardization creates later problems.
- Ensure that all the people involved in processes have up-to-date and easily accessible knowledge about their accountabilities; using an intranet can help this education process.

This is even more true where some of your processes are outsourced, and RBS found this particularly difficult as only part processes have been outsourced as opposed to end-to-end work. For example, some 'new hire' contracts have been outsourced where the roles are generic and lend themselves well to good technology and case management (which Hewitt Associates have). However, in the initial stages, and given the concerns above, the process would go from line to local HR to HR service centre to Hewitt when the line to Hewitt route was actually the most efficient!

The need to manage accountabilities really comes down to trust. Can the shared services function (virtual or real) be trusted to deliver a robust and sound service to customers who are used to a more hand-holding arrangement? This trust is hard won and easily lost, and this has been true for RBS. One way of managing customers' expectations is to set in train robust monitoring and reporting procedures.

MONITORING AND REPORTING

It does not matter whether the service offered is profit centric, customer centric, transfer priced, a pure cost centre or however financed, although these are decisions that have to be taken relative to the size, scale, business approach and culture of your organization. The RBS is not a huge advocate of large teams of internal resources transfer pricing to the nearest pound all central costs. Therefore, the RBS HR shared services function is managed on a budget/forecast basis and recharged to the income-generating businesses on a headcount prorata basis. That said, regardless of the model, service levels should be created, agreed, monitored and reported.

The RBSG created SLAs around timeliness of process completion (e.g. 48 hours for a new hire contract, 48 hours for a reference response, etc.) and insisted on similar service levels for its suppliers, including Hewitt. At the time of writing, the number of key monthly service levels monitored within shared services exceeds 40, although this encompasses services across benefits, pensions, HR, payroll and training administration, both internally and externally provided.

Whilst there is a real danger of over-reporting, the value of measuring service levels is as much a management tool as a customer service tool, at least to identify key volume trends, productivity levels and potential areas for improvement. Chapter 9 informs the reader of some of the pitfalls and options, but their value makes them worth the effort.

All the service levels are collated into a single management pack shared with the HR leadership team and, at a lower level, each of the areas (training, HR/payroll, benefits, pensions) shares its more detailed data with their relevant customer stakeholders (e.g. pensions service levels are signed off by, and reported to, the board of trustees). This pack also includes not only service levels but a more balanced set of measures using the scorecard methodology. Other key measures are costs, headcount, productivity, customer surveys, staff surveys, project milestone delivery and complaints.

Whilst somewhat detailed, this section has reviewed the design issues that face any new shared services function, and whilst the content will differ from organization to organization, hopefully the value in some of the activities undertaken by RBS will prove useful. Of course, the design is easy compared with actually getting the thing set up and, whilst some of the design issues also give rise to implementation concerns, the next section considers some of the more critical implementation issues.

4   Implementation

The high-level design signalled more overarching issues for implementation including:

- how to embed the structure and its fit with the rest of HR
- what the issues would be if outsourcing whole or part processes
- how the proposed solution can be 'sold' to the customer and some of the change management issues that arise
- the importance of mapping processes and documenting specific accountabilities, and keeping these fresh in the minds of all involved parties
- making sure that all key measures are known and reported to relevant stakeholders through regular updates.

However, there are some more specific implementation issues to consider within the shared services function, namely:

- communication
- resourcing
- training/education
- pilot/phasing.

This section documents how RBS approached these issues.

COMMUNICATION

One of the key themes of this book is the importance of communication and this was no less an issue in the set-up of the shared services function in RBS. The communication needed to manage the following stakeholder groups:

- customer (line managers and employees)
- HR
- HR shared services function
- outsourced partners (where applicable)
- other key stakeholders.

Whilst one approach may be to take each group individually, RBS used different communication channels and media to hit different groups in different ways. The profusion of communication thus should have enabled all relevant parties to be similarly informed. Key communication channels used were:

- Intranet – the launch of the RBS HR site was used as a platform to inform HR staff (on the private HR intranet site) and line managers/employees of all the new processes that needed to be followed with some use of on-line forms for simple transactions (e.g. change of address). Whilst this was the forerunner of many 'e-HR'-type vehicles now profuse in organizations, at the time its main *raison d'être* was simple information provision. As many readers will know, the additional value is that good use of an intranet can minimize the number of telephone calls to the shared service function on simple issues such as holiday entitlement or maternity policies.

- Bank magazine – this was used to profile the high-level service of the HR*direct* (outsourced call centre), the intranet site and the set-up of the service centre. This is not a good medium for detailed procedures but was good for highlighting the changes and directing people to the relevant materials.
- Business communication channels – the Retail networks did not have 'on-line' communication channels, so business sponsored launch packs with details on process changes etc. were sent to branch managers with the HR*direct* phone number to reinforce any issues that may arise.
- Payslip messaging – the creation of the HR service centre and outsourcing of more calls to HR*direct* was flagged using simple messaging on payslips to better direct queries and general information to the right channel.
- Business-facing HR – as part of the overall HR change programme, HR business partners were challenged with getting their businesses on board with the new approach (with mixed success – see later).
- More detailed workshops were undertaken for the key staff involved who were to work in the HR Shared Services Centre and this is covered more fully in the training evaluation section below.

The key message arising from the experience of RBS was the continued use of the champions identified in the current-state analysis some six months earlier. As these practitioners had been engaged throughout, the value of the communication was enhanced by their personal beliefs of why things had to change. Hindsight would observe that more use of the people involved at the outset would have been even more advantageous.

The RBS did not, however, spend much time educating senior colleagues as to the reasons and benefits; this was left to the generic communication materials described above. Again with hindsight, some of the later problems may well have been better managed through targeted communication to the senior team, although at the time this was not thought useful and may have raised more issues than it was trying to solve. One key reason was the general 'immaturity' that HR perceived existed in how HR could transform itself more generally across the senior team.

A final communication trick was to seek recognition externally through articles, awards and academic reviews of what had been achieved to enhance the reputation externally but also to help people internally identify with something successful – even if the reality had its issues. The RBS won a *Personnel Today* award in 1999 for its approach to outsourcing and was a finalist in the same competition for use of the intranet soon after the launches described above. Innovative ways of communicating to all relevant stakeholders is a necessity to try and embed change – especially where many of the targets are at best sceptical.

RESOURCING

The case study considered in detail the current-state analysis in terms of its people with the outputs of the assessment process and development activity, which, whilst aimed at the 'consulting' side of HR, did give rise to assessments of people whose skills would be better employed in the shared services function. This was especially true of the management/supervisory team of the service centre where the assessments had leaned towards a more transactional/operational strength than genuine business-facing consulting.

As has also been mentioned, the payroll and pensions administration functions were largely in place given their specific technical skill requirements. That said, it was also true that the customer focus in these units was limited and, given that the switch from administration function to 'service' function was a deliberate shift in emphasis, not just in name, there was still work to be done in these areas.

The main aspect of resourcing then was the creation of the HR service centre and, of course, agreement with Hewitt as to the extent of resources engaged to carry out RBS HR processes. Additionally, resourcing is not just about skills, it is also true for quantity and structure and these two have been difficult issues to grasp.

Clarity of overall HR delivery strategy, too, has an impact on resourcing and, while it was not known at the time, the biggest difficulty of all has been the acquisition and integration of NatWest which created a need for a major rethink.

In summary the key issues and actions were:

- HR delivery strategy – the general direction was to seek more and more opportunities to outsource given the limited scope and scale of the internal mandate at the time, and the continued fight for technology investment relative to those organizations whose business it is to invest in technology. Many suppliers in payroll, benefits and HR processing seek to reinvest about 5 per cent of revenues back into technology. These investments by HR outsourcing specialists will never be matched by organizations whose business is banking, chemicals, pharmaceuticals or telecoms (even allowing for recent developments). From a resourcing perspective then, more temporary and fixed-term resources were used in the internal service centre (over 50 per cent), whereas more long-term resourcing took place within Hewitt.

- Quantity – this has been the most singularly difficult issue to manage since inception. So many issues are 'in play' and reliance on good supply chain management is fundamental. There are too many variables to document in this case study but the key issue is work volume predictability. Even when the set-up follows a current-state analysis, what detail there might be (and there was little in RBS's case) on past volumes, for example new hire contracts, are by definition historical. While this was a guide, the in-built assumption was steady state. Anyone who has studied the history of RBSG in the last two years will know the reality has been far from steady state! Even predicting how many people will join and leave the Group (and these are by far and away the biggest cost drivers for HR shared service centres) is not easy, let alone resourcing to manage those volumes. Recently, better work-flow management, productivity measures and management tools have been implemented. For anyone setting up a shared services function now, the investment in good resource management tools is a must. That it is only an internal function is not an excuse.

- Structurally – the approach taken in the shared services function has been to segment broad activity by 'commodity', i.e. pensions, payroll, HR, training and benefits services. This gives clarity to the management, segments expertise but by being under a single management structure can lead to efficiencies in shared learnings and infrastructure. A more integrated model may suit other organizations – at set-up it was not right for RBS. There is a fundamental issue that is created as a result, though, and that is to ensure the customer does not become a victim of HR's own demands, i.e. a new member of staff should not have to worry about which bit of HR does what, that the 'commodity' areas connect to enable the customer to have an integrated experience is key. One way to manage this is to put a common 'helpline' front end which can interface with all the different parties. This has not been in place to date for RBS but is now on the horizon.

Many readers will consider other resourcing issues as key. The ones described above, and some of the actions to manage them, were key for RBS. However, this section has only really covered the overall structure, the mix, the volume and some high-level skill issues. The training needs analysis and interventions need to be added to complete the shared services function's capability to deliver.

TRAINING/EDUCATION

There is only a fine line between training and education and the communication issues described earlier in this chapter of the book. This part therefore only considers the training issues contained within delivering the service from the central shared services perspective rather then the customer engagement, HR communication and line manager engagement already covered.

There were three key tenets to the training issues on the creation of the shared service function of RBS:

- customer service training for the technical areas already in place
- technical training for the centralized HR processing unit
- technical and orientation training for the outsourced part of the shared service function.

For the customer services element, this was conducted for the payroll, pensions and training administrators who were being repositioned as a core part of a shared services function from being traditional administration units. The teams had a wealth of good technical knowledge relevant to their vocation but investment in learning telephone skills, good questioning and a customer ethos were challenges to be overcome. Each team was involved in customer service training and a wider education programme about the reasons for creating a shared services function and this proved useful if not conclusive. With hindsight, a mix of technical and dedicated customer-orientated staff may have been a more productive solution.

For the new HR processing unit, much of the effort was spent on embedding processes into roles, into training plans and into the day-to-day work. This was effected through two approaches: using experienced people, released early from their previous employment in the devolved teams to spend a few weeks dedicated to the training of the new resources and, second, phasing the work so that there was some overcapacity where spare time could be used to further train on processes 'on the job'. Both were successful.

The third element was that RBS staff were dedicated to train the outsourced employees on both the deep technical issues but, perhaps more importantly, also spent some time on what RBS is like. This latter approach had been used with some success when the outsourced flexible benefits scheme administration had been set up some 18 months earlier. This true partnership approach proved useful once more in helping HR*direct* embed itself as a perceived extension of the HR resource in the Group as opposed to a third party.

With the increased scale, following the acquisition of NatWest, much of what was done originally had to be redone and thus perhaps proved once more the value of taking time to train and educate those responsible for delivering the service. The phased approach allowed room for this to happen, although some might prefer a 'big bang'. The pros and cons from the RBS experience are reviewed below.

PILOT/PHASING

In Chapter 6 of this book the debate about whether to phase a launch or whether to create a 'big bang' is considered in detail. From the experience of RBS, phasing is more beneficial as it does not assume a blank sheet of paper, acknowledges that customers do not stop needing support across many HR processes for a few weeks nor, perhaps most importantly, allows the necessary refinements to be made before all customer groups are on board. However, the risks are that if it is not quite going to plan, and RBS had some teething problems (but then most do), latter phase customers have ready-made excuses not to join something that they might have been against anyway. This was not true for RBS but did create some debate.

The RBS split the work into both processes and customer groups to allow well-managed transition, although the work took some six to nine months to completely migrate. The affected customer base (some 22 000 staff) is probably a bit light for such a long take-up period, however the key mitigating factor was volume underestimation (thus capacity was reached quicker than expected and new recruits were required). This transfer of work also happened at the time that RBS was successful in its bid for NatWest and thus the shared services set-up did take a back seat.

So, for RBS phasing had a number of advantages but also gave rise to some concerns. The real question though is, has it been a success? The final chapter of the book considers that question. However, before doing so, it is probably worth highlighting what has happened since the journey to shared services commenced. This will enable the final analysis not just to be considered in isolation as some theoretical exercise but to be based more on the reality of life that often affects any business change.

5   Recent events

The shared services implementation commenced in earnest in spring 1999 with the launch of the intranet, some initial outsourcing and the amalgamation of pensions, benefits, training, payroll and HR processing into HR (shared) services. This was supported by HR*direct*, a front-end outsourced telephony capability serving 22 000 employees on a myriad of policy and procedural questions. Additionally, some new hire contracts, referencing, maternity processing and structured questionnaires for leavers and joiners were all outsourced. This took about 12 months to conclude.

During late 1999, the intention of RBSG to acquire NatWest was made public and after a somewhat protracted battle with the board of NatWest and the Edinburgh-based Bank of Scotland, the acquisition process concluded in mid-February 2000. The overall business opportunities for the enlarged Group have been well documented. The main implication for HR was how to integrate the larger-scale insourced capability into both the existing RBS HR strategy and infrastructure supporting over 100 000 employees.

Other key issues that arose from the transaction were:

- The acquisition was grounded on a new operating model for the Group, a centralized manufacturing base for *all* businesses. This model was championed by the new Group

Chief Executive (Fred Goodwin) and was seen as the major tenet of the £600 million or so 'de-duplication' savings identified in the bid. HR's contribution to this de-duplication was not inconsiderable and centred around the profusion of HR systems, processes and administration functions that existed Group-wide, in essence, a larger and more complicated rationale to the one that faced RBS two years earlier.

- The bid also centred on speed. A standing parameter of the bid was that RBS policy, practice and infrastructure would be used unless proven differently. The upside is that this negates lengthy systems analysis on which is better whilst continuing to pay dual licence fees, development costs and so on. Even if this meant lost customer functionality, this was the first objective. This was also true for HR. NatWest had the SAP payroll system with greater functionality but with some implementation pain. The quicker, easier and financially more viable option was to replace the NatWest payroll with a version of the RBS Unipay system. The issue for the shared services function was that lost functionality meant some customer dissatisfaction and also additional resources in the HR Service Centre.

- The third main consideration was the overall direction and strategy. What had been an obvious move towards increasing outsourcing in HR because of issues identified earlier in this case study was now less clear cut. NatWest had a very well run HR service centre, based in Manchester serving over 60 000 employees. The training administration function served the same population from London. Pensions and benefits administration was based in Croydon serving over 100 000 customers, both active staff and pensioners. This internal capability to deal with scale had never existed in RBS, thus the base point was rewritten.

- The final concern was how the integration of NatWest in RBS would be supported within the HR environment generally, and by the shared services function in particular. This included the myriad of policy and procedural changes, the changes to terms and conditions for over 50 000 employees, the vast training effort required to support the business IT system migration, the whole restructuring effort including recruitment, retention and, where applicable, redundancy; in short, and as any reader who has been through a major integration will testify, the vast increase of work that HR has to support to embed the two organizations into a new Group.

These four major issues are supported by many further ones such as, how does RBS build an ongoing acquisition/integration capability. Indeed, at the time of writing, RBS has concluded a further six transactions including further growth in the USA with transactions that now take the number of US employees to over 11 000. Thus, a total rethink of the shared services strategy has been undertaken and a revised way forward articulated. However, much of the old strategy has been retained as some of the key reasons still exist:

- Technology resource for HRIS issues is even more scarce and far less of a priority to the business technology issues – this lends itself to more outsourcing.
- The business model now gives executive remit to create a single Group HR 'manufacturing' capability including systems, processing and services.
- The internal delivery capability will be considered in tandem with any external possibilities once the final major HR integration activity is complete in late 2002.
- The value of internal measures, reporting and management systems is even more transparent than it was preacquisition.
- The foundations of the RBS approach and the internal scale at NatWest have been merged to better position for the businesses' ever-growing needs.

Thus, shared services is even more attractive than it was before. Indeed, new streams of activity in information provision, policy advice, recruitment, expatriate support, project management, business acquisition and integration, and HR risk management are now included in the shared services remit.

So with these recent developments, and restated ambition, the shared services function is set to grow, supporting over 100 000 employees, seven major business streams (such as Direct Line, Ulster Bank and the two retail networks in the UK) and in total over 200 000 lives once pensioners, deferred pensioners, potential employees and temporary staff are included. The future is set to be challenging, but what has been learnt and what would the verdict so far be on its success?

6   Conclusion

The key issues and conclusions from the RBS experience have been integrated into Chapter 9, which looks at what pitfalls arise in the creation of an HR shared services function and offers many suggestions as to how to avoid and/or manage them.

Certainly the creation of an HR shared services approach in RBS, whilst not yet complete even in 2002, has been positive. Some key reasons are:

1 Shared services gives a single point of accountability for HR transactions and process ownership. Once in place, further change is less difficult.
2 The focus on shared services in RBS has allowed real measures of performance, quality, efficiency and productivity to be understood and customer feedback gauged. Again this helps for continuous improvements across all dimensions.
3 For integration activities, a shared services function is critical to enable scale effectiveness and a production-line approach quickly to be established. The RBS shared services function has supported over 40 000 changes of terms and conditions since the acquisition within the first 28 months of the integration.
4 By 2004, a full realization of significant efficiency savings and value of the shared services function will be possible.

Hopefully these positive statements give the reader a greater insight into some of the issues faced in the last four years within the now expanded RBS and why it is correctly considered the right thing to have done even though the complete realization of the benefits are still 18 months away. Yes some costs have gone down, some have increased. Yes some service levels may have dipped, but only in perception terms as we do not know the original service levels because no base case data on service turnarounds existed. The organization comprises now over 100 000 employees not 22 000 and recruitment volumes are volatile to say the least. Continued progress against the strategy, vigilance of SLA standards and performance, consistent communication to key stakeholders and so on all need to be used to convince any sceptics of the success so far.

The bottom line is that there is no single measure to prove the success or otherwise of shared services. What is needed is the faith to see the job through and create a single centre of excellence for all HR 'manufacturing' activity for the Group and review the benefits at the end of the progress of change, not midway through.

9 *Pitfalls and solutions*

Whilst there are many reasons to adopt HR shared services, which we explored in Chapter 2, and many benefits to be found, you should not be under any illusion that there are difficulties to be faced. Nobody should think of shared services as the solution to all your problems. It may well, indeed should, reduce costs. It ought to give you the chance to improve standards and develop a service ethos. It can help to reposition HR and give the function more flexibility to respond to organizational change. Yet there are difficult issues and tensions that you will have to deal with. This chapter aims to pass on the experiences of others so that you can be prepared to meet these challenges.

Potential problems

SKILLS AND DEVELOPMENT

There are implications for skills and development in the introduction of shared services. These are issues that affect the initial job design and those that impact development over the longer term. There are matters to be confronted both in terms of de-skilling and up-skilling.

The main risk in de-skilling occurs in the design of some administrative jobs. There is the danger that, for reasons of efficiency, they are stripped down to the point where they become extremely tedious to perform. An example of this is where the person has nothing to do but enter changes to employee records. This problem is more acute where staff have previously undertaken a wider range of tasks. For example, personnel assistants in small teams serving a single business unit will have had more variety than they may have in shared service centres where they are asked to do a narrower range of tasks. They may have looked after payroll/records changes, relocation, maternity pay, benefits administration, etc.

Moreover, there are potential difficulties with future career development if lower-graded staff do not build the expertise (possible in more generalist roles in traditional HR units) that allows them to fill more senior positions later. There is too big a jump between the administrative role and one with supervisory responsibility or expertise in a subject area.

At the other end of the jobs' hierarchy, organizations may be asking too much of the business-facing HR managers in concentrating exclusively on strategy and change management, having removed their operational *raison d'être*. There is a real question of whether HR managers, used to running an operational team, can suddenly successfully switch to being a strategic business partner. Previously, the HR manager has derived his/her power from ensuring the smooth running of people-related activities. Now the HR manager has to use a different set of skills that rely upon influencing without a resource or operational base, but through professional insight and by acting more like a broker of services than a deliverer. The skill required of the new HR manager is that of successfully co-ordinating the various players so that the business gets a coherent service. There is also the question of whether the HR manager knows how to be strategic, what interventions to make. In some organizations there may be the injunction to 'get strategic' with little help over understanding the nature of a strategic contribution. Whilst some may welcome the chance to focus their work on matters of greater significance, other HR managers may feel a loss of power and control. Customers, too, may fail to appreciate or support this change. They may be continually trying to dumb down the HR manager's contribution. It needs a confident and assertive HR manager to keep focused on high-level work and avoid the distraction of solving every problem raised by line colleagues. Yet at the same time the manager must be sufficiently responsive that important operational HR issues do not get neglected.

EXAMPLE 9.1

One financial services organization had been developing a shared services model for some five years before it was decided that it was not working. The principal problem was the opposition of HR staff themselves. HR managers felt that, in particular, they had insufficient control over payroll administration. They were removed from the decision-making process that seemed too centralized under corporate control. Previously, they were allowed discretion and interpretation in the application of policy. Standardization brought welcome consistency to the organization, but both denied HR managers a role and made for less interesting work for the administrative staff themselves. The latter also became increasingly frustrated at the narrow definition of their role and the restricted opportunities for career development.

EFFECTIVE ACCOUNTABILITY IN A SEGMENTED SERVICE

The issues here concern responsibility and boundary management in the context of a segmented service, i.e. one with different, separate strands of service for different activities.

One set of problems may present themselves at the interface between operational support to business, delivered close to the business unit, and administration of HR tasks. So the HR manager in the business unit may be responsible for the personnel services delivered to their business unit managers but have no control over the work if it is done in a shared service centre, managed by another HR team. Service level agreements may govern the nature of the service, but often the monitoring measures are more to do with process than outcome. This may lead to the absence of effective accountability, as the HR manager denies responsibility for aspects of the service to the customer, and yet he/she is frequently the interface between the business and the services centre.

Boundary management issues are also likely to occur elsewhere in a heavily segmented service. For example, if the corporate centre is in charge of policy and the business-facing HR manager with delivery, where does policy formation end and implementation begin? If you are developing a performance management process, how do you ensure that the learning you achieve through operating the process gets fed back into policy design?

There are potentially communication difficulties, again where there are numerous discrete activities, each organizationally separate. This is a perennial problem, but harder if the boundaries between parts of the function (i.e. corporate centre, HR manager and shared services organization) are too rigidly drawn.

Segmentation can also pose problems where the operation of a policy and the administration of it are too separate. Are you able to pick up employee or management issues that those handling the administration of, say, a relocation or maternity policy uncover?

Additionally, the process of change can often blur any boundaries that do exist and only serve to add to the confusion and frustration. Clear management of the overall objective and journey can help minimize the frustrations, as can recognition that it will occur in the first place.

EXAMPLE 9.2

One organization found that there was a lack of clarity in the boundary between policy development and policy execution. The former activity was located in the corporate centre; the latter in the shared services centre. We were told that the problem was containable only because those in both departments had had previous experience of working together. Their good personal relationships got them through. The structure was an impediment to a good process, not a facilitator of it.

RECOGNITION OF THE VALUE OF ADMINISTRATIVE WORK

Organizations have the aspiration that by diminishing the importance of administrative activities, the HR function can concentrate on higher value-added work. Whilst not always meaning to suggest that administrative work is of little consequence, people (especially consultants) talk of 'getting rid' of the transactional in a sort of 'out of sight, out of mind' way. There are two dangers in this approach. Administrative personnel work is vital to the smooth running of any organization. If people are not paid on time or paid incorrectly, then there is understandable disgruntlement. Moreover, if employee records are a mess, not only are staff irritated, but any attempt to monitor employee patterns (e.g. the growth of part-time or temporary staff) is doomed to failure. It also makes HR vulnerable to the charge that if it cannot run a payroll successfully, how can it claim to be able to develop the competencies of staff or whatever.

The second consequence is that those HR staff working on administrative tasks see themselves as second-class citizens doing jobs that are little regarded. This affects morale as well as recruitment to these posts. You may find that the poorer staff are the ones parked in administrative roles, partly because this is the perception of others who avoid such work.

EXAMPLE 9.3

In one organization it was said that administrative work lacked 'kudos'. In another it was claimed that administrative staff felt they were 'underdogs', always visualized as at the bottom of the picture and never described as professionals. In both organizations recruiting to these posts proved difficult.

Neglecting the importance of the knowledge and experience of those who had performed administrative roles in the past can also lead to problems. These people have the technical expertise in HR policies and procedures. They have established good relationships with customers based on knowing the people and the culture. Ignoring this factor in resourcing shared service centre posts can lead to deterioration in the quality of services. This is clearly an issue in the transition to your new arrangements, but also in the retention of staff once the shared services centre is up and running.

This is becoming increasingly apparent and the recognition of the criticality of either the shared services function or the tight management of external suppliers is becoming more understood. The concept that many value accurate and timely HR processing means that any attempt to dumb-down the service can have significant implications to the overall reputation of HR.

INTEGRATING HR

Segmenting HR services helps make clear to customers what they can expect from different parts of the function. Combining work into a shared service centre has advantages in resource optimization and in improving learning within a particular team. There are, however, risks involved:

- Deciding to whom resources should be allocated, especially in a project organization. The process should be more transparent than in the past, but the emphasis on prioritization can leave individual business units dissatisfied with the result.
- The project-based approach to functional support, which means that HR completes the task and moves on. In itself this is a good thing, ensuring that resources are well managed, but it can result in the consultant not seeing the work through to a real conclusion.
- The right hand does not know what the left hand is doing. So, far from offering an integrated service, the line is presented with a disparate offering.
- Consultancy is given in a context-free manner. In other words, because those in the consultancy pool have no particular knowledge of any business, they give generalized rather than tailored advice. This may mean that local issues are ignored.
- Some personnel staff become detached from the business. They provide services to it but in an indirect manner – they lack both the feel of what is going on in the business and commitment to it. Personnel staff do not always know what is happening on the ground and are very reliant on being kept well informed.
- There is poor organizational learning across groups. Problems which are identified in one area are not picked up elsewhere. Thus, those handling the administration of relocation may be aware of individual difficulties that policy-makers should know. Helplines may discover a series of disputes in the same business unit that centre on a particular manager but, as they are organizationally divorced from the problem, they have to convince others of the importance of the issue.
- Boundary disputes occur over who is responsible for what. Those charged with implementing policy complain that they are given insufficient guidance and have themselves to flesh out policies. Helplines pass problems to others if they become too complicated, but specialists may believe that insufficient is being done in escalating only the really difficult cases.

EXAMPLE 9.4

A transport company dealt with the multiplicity of requests for project resources by setting up a corporate HR committee to vet work proposals. The committee received bids from HR business managers. It decided whether (a) it was a project that should be supported, and if so (b) whether it should be done in house or (c) be resourced externally. If the task was to be done by the internal project team, it was given a level of priority. Clearly, those who did well out of this process found it to be satisfactory. HR business managers, and their business management teams more so, took a dim view of having their ideas knocked back.

EFFICIENCY VERSUS CHOICE IN CUSTOMER SERVICE

If the shared services concept is distinguished by the fact that it is customer focused, what type and nature of services will the customer want and will tensions arise over what HR thinks it is appropriate to offer? One answer is that in the shared service model this is not a problem so long as the customer is prepared to pay. However, there are a number of issues here:

- Can line managers choose to buck the devolvement trend, i.e. insist on HR participation even in activities deemed to be their responsibility (e.g. recruitment or discipline)? This may be a question of managers lacking time or skills, in which case remedial action can be taken. But it could be a more philosophical objection to HR withdrawing its expertise, and this will require serious debate.
- Is the customer always right in deciding on a particular course of action? Is HR merely giving advice which the line manager can accept or reject, or upholding corporate values or principles that the manager has to accept? Clearly, the answer depends upon the issue; it may be matter of interpretation. A trusting relationship between the parties will avoid most problems, but this is not always present. The difficulty is that there are likely to be a multiplicity of models in the line management and HR relationship – a client/contractor for certain services, a strategic partner in other circumstances and acceptor of the guardian's direction on matters of corporate principles. This, though, requires some sophistication.
- Does corporate efficiency have a higher value than customer choice? Part of the point of having shared services is to obtain economies of scale. These will be lost, or at least reduced, if the customer keeps choosing to be different. You then get the multiplicity of redundancy compensation schemes or performance-related pay systems. You need to decide which policies should be treated as commodities, where the lowest delivery price should be sought, and which can be designed to meet specific business need. So the organization can distinguish between those services that are deemed to be common (e.g. the payroll and records system), from those which are optional (recruitment, relocation, etc.) where the business unit can take the corporate service, do it themselves or buy from elsewhere.
- There are still potential difficulties in what those wanting a common service mean by commonality. One business unit might want a high-volume recruitment service with little sophistication, whereas another business unit might want tailor-made recruitment with

intensive contact with each candidate. Services can, of course, be adjusted to do both, but it does leave the service provider in a position of having to juggle to meet customer needs.

- Especially if SLAs are used, there is a danger of distortion in the services provided. HR staff have targets to meet and these are the matters that get dealt with. Other matters not covered by the SLA get ignored. This means that longer-term or more complex issues get sidelined. It may also lead to too much emphasis being put on selling products, with insufficient attention to the content.

HR'S ROLE WITH RESPECT TO EMPLOYEES

In the desire to be aligned with the business and to devolve as much activity as they can to line managers, some HR departments either deny they have a role in relation to employees or relegate it to a purely care and maintenance state. This might mean providing them with basic services, but not seeing it as the function's role to understand or promote the employee viewpoint in management circles. If this is the line you take, the result may be that you are not equipped to explain to senior management how employees will respond to business initiatives. Ignorance of the employee perspective, may make you less effective in facilitating cultural change. HR staff may be seen as remote to employees or not to be trusted, and therefore not appropriate as a conduit to senior management.

The danger in this approach is that HR's aspiration to be a strategic partner has to be based on its distinctive contribution, that of its knowledge of people – what makes them tick, what motivates them to contribute to organizational performance, what inclines them to stay or leave the organization, etc. If it has no special expertise, what right has it to sit alongside finance, marketing or production?

Difficulties in getting a feel for the organizational temperature can be exacerbated where there is little face-to-face contact with managers or employees. This can happen if impersonal media (like computers or telephones) dominate the means of service provision. Where employees are widely dispersed in small units, this may be understandable. Indeed, there may be more contact with HR in this way than in the past, but there is less reason in large offices or factories.

These problems will be exacerbated if customers believe the existing HR model is acceptable and do not see the need for change. You may be able to convince them of the improvement in service if you work hard at your communication. Should you have to override their objections because of wider organizational benefits, you cannot expect managers especially to give you an easy ride or the benefit of the doubt if there are service hiccups. This may lead some managers to find ways of asserting their independence and testing the model. In these circumstances, the tension between efficiency and customer responsiveness may become even more noticeable.

DUMPING ON LINE MANAGERS

In the attempt to get HR to become more strategic, some organizations have combined the introduction of shared services with making managers more responsible for people management. Part of the means of being more strategic is through the function freeing itself from mundane work. It has often sought to do this by passing these tasks to line managers to do – to record information, to run processes like sickness absence. Some tasks transferred to the line may be of higher value, for example managing performance-related pay reviews, interviewing for recruitment or conducting performance management processes.

Nevertheless, devolution has not, it seems, been without problems. While some managers have welcomed their increased freedom to act, others have floundered, requiring HR staff to come to bail them out. Difficulties from the managerial perspective seem to centre on a lack of time or skills to undertake new work. This might include being unaware of the limits of their authority. From a corporate standpoint, there has been concern about a lack of consistency across the organization in people management, with some unjustifiable differences in employee treatment emerging. There has also been resistance from personnel staff to losing control over activities that were once seen to be under their aegis.

EXAMPLE 9.5

Compaq had had a policy of devolving HR activities to line managers. This had not proved to be wholly successful because many managers were not sufficiently trained or skilled to fulfil the role they were asked to cover. The result was that senior HR staff found themselves drawn into dealing with employee problems raised by the staff themselves. This meant that HR was distracted from its aim to be more involved in bigger people management issues. (IDS, 2001)

We suggest that great care is taken in considering who should undertake HR activities. If the devolved work is mundane, line managers may rightly query why they should be expected to do the work. Or, if they do not quibble, they may well create new armies of clerks to do the work, thereby reducing overall organizational cost-efficiency. If the work is more complex, there is the question of whether managers have the competence to perform the tasks.

Of course, you can offer training and support to deal with any skill gaps. But the problem may be deeper. The people management skills in your organization may be inadequate because the management selection process does not look for people management skill; it may emphasize technical ability or a track record of delivering results. Again, you can use your appraisal system to identify competency deficiencies and seek to improve levels of, say, interpersonal skills. And you can offer resources to help undertake some of the work, if this still fits your model and cost plan.

Ensuring that managers should exercise their right to manage has also made devolution more problematic for HR managers. How do we give the line greater authority for people management and yet ensure they exercise their responsibilities in such a way that does not harm the organization overall? The ambiguity of HR's position is apparent. It seeks to facilitate change, and perform the role of adviser to the line manager, but it finds it difficult to stop adopting a policing role. It seems hard for HR to avoid being 'props and cops' (an American manager quoted in Eisenstat, 1996) supporting the line to solve its problems and acting as the corporate enforcer to prevent managers breaking the rules.

Nevertheless the new dawn of the e-HR capabilities, if implemented from the users' perspective, should help significantly in reducing both the transfer of administrative work and ignorance of personnel policy and practice. The latter can be 'hardwired' into processes so that the information is readily available. For example, if a line manager does not know the overtime rates and would have had to check first before entering into a form for submission, e-HR can build in the rates automatically and include any counter-signature facility. Not only does it remove activity from HR, it can speed up the process for line managers. However, even if you remove the burden of paperwork/bureaucracy, will line managers still prove capable of managing their employees effectively? Will they more readily assume accountability for their staff? The case is not yet totally proven.

The issues of devolvement are largely solvable, but you need to recognize the potential problems and have the means to deal with them. If this is not done, you will find that either the standard of people management will deteriorate or HR will be drawn back into activities from which it has sought to withdraw.

TECHNOLOGICAL TROUBLES

Some shared services models require large-scale capital investment in order to obtain the necessary technological infrastructure. This might mean refurbishment of the existing HRIS, or the purchase of a new one. It might require investment in telephony to support a call centre or IVR system. Intranets may need to be created. Communication systems may have to be upgraded to facilitate information transfer between locations. Sums involved may not be trivial. Moreover, there is the expertise to develop the technology that may have to be hired or contracted in.

Some organizations do not have a good track record in delivering technology investment successfully. What are the dangers?

- You may be unrealistic over what can be delivered and by when. You may suffer from over-expectation of the speed and nature of technological improvement. This might simply be due to an overambitious timetable for implementation. If this simply means a delay in start-up, you may be able to cope reasonably easily. Much more problematic are situations where changes are made elsewhere in the organization, predicated on the assumption that systems and software are in place, when this is not the case. An example would be where cuts in staff numbers are made in HR administration based on the assumption that employee self-service is up and running. Thus fewer HR staff may be available to make, say, adjustments to employee records, but the volume of work has not diminished because staff are not doing this themselves. The result is that the quality of the service deteriorates. The shared service centre gets off to a bad start, allowing critics to rubbish the new concept.

EXAMPLE 9.6

On the basis of its own experience a media company believes that organizations should be 'realistically sceptical' about how quickly technology will work and deliver intended results. When it implemented shared services it did so together with a new HRIS. HR numbers were reduced with the expectation that the new technology would save time on many tasks and hence jobs. The function tended to overpromise what the change would deliver. When this happened more slowly than the advance publicity, frustration built up for both HR staff and customers. The former found that the technology was not releasing time but absorbing it; the latter saw the standard of service dip as the HR staff struggled to cope.

- You may have assumed IT support for your technological changes that does not materialize. This may happen if you outsource your HR IT systems and the service provider does not deliver as specified or as you hoped but had not specified in the contract. The problem may occur without outsourcing. Internal IT support may be limited by a shortage of resource, expertise or interest – HR IT systems may not have a high priority in the greater scheme of things.

EXAMPLE 9.7

One company found that the delivery of new desktop personal computers for managers, vital for the rollout of the self-service operation, was last minute to say the least. It meant that managers had limited time for training and familiarization with the new system. This put undue pressure on the project team and risked the quality of the launch of the new approach to HR.

- A more fundamental difficulty you may experience is that some of the supposed time-saving technology does not deliver. Systems may crash frequently, do not work at all, or do not do what they were supposed to do. This might be because of serious flaws in the system design or, more likely, due to problems in the way the system was set up. Again, if staffing reductions were based on the time-saving benefits of technology, e.g. from using computer text scanning devices, that did not materialize, then services will probably suffer. Or the benefits of technology might not be enjoyed. For example, having data on computer allows it to be shared among a number of users. If the technology fails, line managers or different HR teams may be denied access to vital information.

The lesson you should draw from these examples is that organizations must be cautious in project management and in the selection of computer products. The first may be easier than the second to accomplish. Computer sales people can be very persuasive. HR may be pushed by other parts of the organization towards choosing particular solutions. The risk is that you end up with unsuitable technology that does not deliver what you want, either now or in the future.

One benefit of outsourcing is that you can minimize this risk by passing the activity to a provider who will need to continue to invest in developing technologies from which the client benefits. However, outsourcing adds another link, a more complicated one, to the chain. Data may have to be passed to a third party for payroll or record entries. Changes in HR policy may need to be reflected in adjustments to these systems. The risk of errors creeping in may grow.

EXAMPLE 9.8

BP is now (late 2001) reviewing whether the outsourcing of its administrative functions should be extended beyond the UK and the USA. This is largely because employees seem reluctant to use the new e-HR technology. Managers believe that they may have gone too far in automating its HR activities. This includes the standardization of reward policies that was not achievable or even desirable. HR costs have risen because traditional forms of contact are running alongside e-HR. (Higginbottom, 2001)

OUTSOURCING DIFFICULTIES

As we remarked earlier, problems with outsourcing can be experienced at all stages of the process. Those which frequently occur include:

- Contractual (legal) disputes. Organizations have experienced difficulties over the terms of the deal, be it to do with money – what costs are included, what is additional? – or to do with service – what standards were set and what exceptional circumstances are permitted to affect these standards?
- Service problems. This may be because the contractor has overreached what they can deliver. They have devoted insufficient resources. Their management expertise is inadequate.
- Lack of internal expertise to manage contractors. Sometimes managers forget that contracts have to be managed. If all the knowledge and skills are transferred to the contractor, who ensures that the organization is not taken for a ride or to the cleaners?
- Change out of contractors' key staff. Sometimes the problems start soon after the outsourcing deal has gone through. The key players that you expected to see in the supplier's team move on and leave you with a lack of continuity.
- Employee relations issues. These may occur over the terms of the transfer (pensions can be especially problematic as they are not covered by TUPE), selection for transfer or redundancy, employee perceptions of inadequate consultation and insufficient negotiation.
- Unexpected costs. These may arise because of inadequate contract specification at the outset or poor management of the contract during its operation. For example, how many organizations recognize how much the service is costing to deliver before offering it to the external market? Without such information, it is more difficult to look at external bids and take a view on how the contractor can perform the same activities but at a cheaper price, and still make a profit. It means that the contractor can overcharge you or be unable to deliver a quality service at the agreed price. Failure to price the work internally, not only prevents comparisons being made with competitor organizations, but also stops you paring down internal costs before market testing. This means that you cannot challenge whether the service could be performed more cheaply externally or internally.
- The presence of a new bureaucracy to monitor contractor performance. The opposite problem of insufficient monitoring may come about from organizations having to expend excessive amounts of time and energy keeping track of their contractor's performance. These situations can spawn lots of paperwork and form filling. This may be necessary but irksome.
- Being locked into inflexible contracts. Overdetailed and rigorous contracts can suffocate your ability to be flexible to organizational change – unable to respond to technological development or policy alteration without considerable time, effort and cost to create new frameworks.
- Failure to meet the aspirations of customers. This can be a simple or complicated problem. If the contractor fails to deliver what is clearly asked for, then the organization must use whatever means it has at its disposal to get the contractor to perform. Of course, what is expected may be in dispute, as indicated earlier. This may only be an issue of poor communication between contractor and client that can be solved. Or the contract may be badly drafted. A more difficult problem to solve is if you have outsourced the work to save money and have taken the opportunity to lower service levels at the same time. Customers complain about the effect of outsourcing when it is in fact the organization that is to blame. If this is not dealt with honestly, outsourcing gets a worse name and customers are not coached into expecting a reasonable service, at a reasonable price.

DEPERSONALIZATION OF HR PROCESSES

Some of the early complaints from employees about shared services have centred around the loss of face-to-face contact with HR staff. This may have arisen from a number of sources:

- the introduction of a call centre or intranet means that employees may not physically meet HR advisers or, in the case of the intranet, even speak to them
- the devolvement of personnel responsibility to line managers and the exiting of HR from contact with employees on a whole range of issues
- the co-location of services that removes HR presence from a number of sites
- the stripping down of business unit HR resources to the bare minimum with the rest of the staff transferred to a central service centre.

Whatever the cause, and it may be all of the above, there is reason to be concerned if staff complain of a depersonalized service. You should worry on two counts. First, are you satisfied that employee issues are being satisfactorily dealt with or do they lie unresolved? Second, are you sufficiently in touch with employees' views to enable you to use your awareness in management debate.

If you hear the comment made by a manager at Apple, 'My HR representative is not a person, it's a floppy disk' (Eisenstat, 1996, p. 20), there is a risk that cynicism and disenchantment have set in. This may or may not be reflected in their performance. Without going that far, it may be that issues lie unresolved that should be tackled. At worst this might be a potential case of bullying. The employee may not be able to turn to their boss who might be the source of the bullying, or an accomplice to it. Your HR department is a natural place to go, but may be more difficult to use if access is impersonal and relationships have not been built up with HR staff. Some of the questions the individual might raise may be trivial or better dealt with by their manager. In these circumstances a call centre or IT system may be usefully screening out this material. The difficulty is that staff might perceive that they are being fobbed off or not treated as human beings. One senior personnel manager told us that at the bereavement of his own mother he felt the need for a more sensitive and personal approach in handling his question on special leave than was possible from the company's call centre.

The second problem stems from the first: not knowing what is going on in the minds of employees may come from not making your team available to hear employees' problems. This makes it harder to deal with upcoming issues. These may not be the strategic questions that HR aspires to tackle. However, they may be the bread-and-butter matters that interest employees. A good HR department might aspire both to contribute to the leadership of the organization and to tackle bottom-up concerns. It is back to the question of who do you regard as your customers (see page 62). If you include employees then you have to acknowledge what it is they want from HR.

But there are differences of opinion on this subject. An HR director in a high-technology company when asked whether he would outsource his HR administration said that he could not conceive of so doing because it was the main point of connection between employees and the function. The former head of Powergen's HR shared services made a similar point but in terms of the importance of face-to-face contact between HR and its customers. The alternative view held by many consultants and companies is that some HR people 'are almost religious about the notion that the only way to deliver HR services is face to face' to quote Martin James of IBM (Pickard, 2000).

However, it is not an all or nothing decision to modernize technology and reposition the HR function on the one side whilst keeping in touch with employees on the other. As we argued on page 5, you can segment the channels of communication that offer employees personal contact where appropriate and impersonal methods where personal interaction is unnecessary. Experience in the banking industry would probably suggest that people are well used to distinguishing between interacting via the telephone or personal computer for low-value activities (e.g cash withdrawal) and through face-to-face contact for more complex transactions (e.g. mortgage advice) if required. The key point is for you to think through the way services are offered not just from an efficiency perspective, but also from a consumer point of view – and that includes employees and managers.

Getting it right

So what steps can HR management take to improve the chances of success and meet the above problems? Here are 20 ideas based on our experience and the example organizations reported here:

1 Be absolutely resolute in delivering what shared services is intended to deliver in your organization. If cost reduction is the aim, then this should guide your decisions. If quality enhancement is the goal, then strive for service improvement. Either way, establishing 'base case' measures will be invaluable. We would suggest that a balanced approach is likely to be successful and this might be what you argue in design. But once settled on the approach, it needs to be seen through.

2 Ensure that your customers understand under what principles and values you are operating. Specify which policies are sacrosanct and not open to challenge. In other words, spell out HR's governance function.

3 Recognize that HR has a number of different customers (e.g. senior management who determine policy direction, line managers who may purchase services, employees who will consume services, their representatives, external bodies, etc.) with different needs. Do not pretend that in satisfying one customer (e.g. the line manager) you have satisfied them all. Also recognize that not all business units will want the same service. Aim to tailor your offering wherever possible, but in the light of the strategic direction, as indicated above.

4 It is poor psychology to tell your customers what is best for them. It is better to agree what your services will be and what the key deliverables are – in this way the shared services concept is spot on. This may mean standardizing some activities, whilst allowing scope for customization on others.

5 Do not forget to clearly communicate HR processes. Customers need to know how they work. Invest time and effort in using a variety of media in getting your point across. Use what suits your organization best – prompt cards, e-messages, booklets, presentations, videos, etc.

6 Find the most effective and efficient means of delivering quality services. This might be through a shared service centre, an e-solution, devolvement to line managers or via local HR managers. Be pragmatic not dogmatic as to which is the best route for the particular service. (Figure 5.2 may help stimulate this sort of decision-making.)

7 Be equally pragmatic about whether activities should be kept in-house or outsourced.

Decide on a cost/benefit basis over the long term as well as the short term, making sure that quality considerations are given as much emphasis as financial ones.

8 If you outsource, give careful attention to the process of selection, transition and control. This involves:

(a) understanding the nature and cost of what you might wish to outsource

(b) getting to grips with any problem internally before outsourcing

(c) defining the contract carefully

(d) making a considered choice of supplier

(e) communicating carefully with staff directly affected and with customers

(f) establishing adequate, but not excessive, monitoring processes with relevant key performance indicators.

9 Set goals for the shared services function. Give high-level attention to the monitoring of services and reporting them to stakeholders. Specify the key clients and obtain credible measures of whether you are meeting their needs. Service levels, customer feedback, costs and productivity are key. If you do review processes, get the right people involved. You should aim for the virtuous circle that sees service delivery as an integrated activity from start to finish.

10 Spend some time seeing how your HR processes fit together. Without necessarily going the whole hog of completing a business process re-engineering exercise, reconfigure HR to fit with the outputs to the customer. Do not get stuck with structures rooted in history or ones that fit the producer's rather than the consumer's needs.

11 Create an integrated and business-focused function through training (ensuring people know their jobs and what others are doing), by putting a high premium on communication both internally within teams but also across them and by organization (e.g. by aligning your project teams or administrative functions so that they handle the work of specific business units, thereby building up local knowledge, its culture, issues it's facing or the characteristics of its management). Specify escalation procedures clearly.

12 Work hard on skilling the HR managers so that they can make a full contribution to meeting local business unit needs, at the strategic or operational level. Make sure that you select managers with the necessary capability and do not appoint those who are either resistant to the new concept or will fail to adjust to the new role.

13 Devolve responsibilities and proper authority to line managers in appropriate areas, but ensure they are properly trained and have positive support from their HR colleagues through advice, helplines or written guidelines. This may well mean taking the process of devolvement gradually.

14 Try and explore all technology, even if your organization is not a fan of spending resources on HR IT. It need not be 'big bang' technology like e-HR, and in any event e-HR is not the nirvana many believe it is. It helps move some transactions to a cheaper and quicker delivery channel, but phone service and even face-to-face contact are still important. Look at work flow, telephony, scanning and other technologies to try and take the mundane tasks out of processing. Find ways of improving the involvement of managers in personnel work and give employees a greater sense of ownership of their personal information, making it more likely that it will be better maintained. This is where e-HR may help.

15 Whilst trying to encourage employees to use the cheapest media, understand that different access routes suit people in different situations. Telephone contact may be easiest for home or mobile workers, whereas the intranet may be better for those in the

office. In setting access routes, be aware of the disadvantages of impersonal media. Recognize that in some circumstances face-to-face contact may be desirable.

16 Understand that there will be boring, repetitive activities to be undertaken within a shared service centre. Either automate them or ensure that through task rotation people have a variety of things to do. Avoid locking people into narrow, dull jobs – this is a recipe for high wastage rates. Develop creative approaches to job swopping within the shared services centre, between it and other parts of HR and even between the client and contractor organizations (in a partially outsourced environment), to give the employee job variety and better career experience needed for development.

17 Whilst making use of communication technology to keep a disparate team well informed and able to access common data, aim for the highest possible co-location of staff, primarily for reasons of maximizing the chances of sharing and learning.

18 Have the clarity and depth of vision to outlast day-to-day problems. HR people do not like change. Many are threatened by the broad change agenda but see the potential value in the shared services function. Front-line HR staff want to be seen as doing useful work. However, they need help to work out what that means.

19 Try and add more value from transactions by exploring ways of supporting the consulting model. This is not just getting the basics right (and helping business partners understand where its customers can also help in starting processes in an accurate and timely manner). It is also about looking at day-to-day activity and exploring what can be done to add more value. Introduce leavers, joiners and contract rejection questionnaires; this provides a great opportunity to front-facing HR staff to look at the data and compare with staff opinion survey data and provide a richer diagnosis to business leaders of the people issues.

20 Keep on the lookout for changes that will continue to reposition your HR function in the way you wish. This might mean finding opportunities to contribute to the business strategy and exiting from tasks where you cannot add value. Keep your HR colleagues aware of these ambitions.

References

Arkin, A. (1999), 'Return to centre', *People Management*, 6 May.

Arkin, A. (2001), 'Central intelligence', *People Management*, 22 November.

Arkin, A. (2002), 'The package to India', *People Management*, 24 January.

Ashton, C. (2000), *Strategic HR: Aligning Human Resources with Corporate Goals*, London: Business Intelligence. For further information visit www.business-intelligence.co.uk

Ashton, C. (2001), *e-HR Transforming the HR Function*, London: Business Intelligence.

Carter, A. and Robinson, D. (2000), *Employee Returns: Linking HR Performance Indicators to Business Strategy*, Institute for Employment Studies, report 365.

Deeks, E. (2000), 'Self-service is hard work', *People Management*, 23 November.

Dick, P. (2000), Implementing shared services after the HR review'. IIR Shared HR Services Conference, 28 February.

Eisenstat, R.A. (1996), 'What corporate human resources brings to the picnic: four models for functional management', *Organizational Dynamics*, **25** (2), 6–14.

Hammond, D. (2001), 'BAE in export drive,' *People Management*, 25 October.

Higginbottom, K. (2001), 'BP learns outsourcing lesson', *People Management*, 8 November.

The Hunter Group Inc. (2000), *Human Resources Self Service Survey*, Baltimore MD: The Hunter Group Inc.

Incomes Data Services (IDS) (2000), *Outsourcing and HR Administration*, IDS report number 700, December.

Incomes Data Services (IDS) (2001), *HR Service Centres*, IDS report number 707, April.

Industrial Relations Services (1998), *The Evolving HR Function*, **10**, July.

Keep, J. (2001), *Models of HR Provision and the Move Towards Shared Services: Continuing the Emergent Review*, NHSP.

Lentz, S.S. (1996), 'Hybrid organization structures: a path to cost savings and customer responsiveness', *Human Resource Management*, **35**, (4) 453–69.

Pickard, J. (2000), 'Centre of attention', *People Management*, 6 July.

Reilly, P. (1999), *Back Office or Shared Service and the Re-alignment of HR*, Institute for Employment Studies, report 368.

Reilly, P. (2000), *Flexibility at Work: Balancing the Interests of Employer and Employee*, Aldershot: Gower.

Reilly, P. and Tamkin, P. (1996), *Outsourcing: A Flexible Option for the Future?* Institute for Employment Studies, report 320.

Rosenbaum, A. (1999), 'Back offices and the euro', *Human Resources*, June.

Trapp, R. (2001), 'Of mice and men', *People Management*, 28 June.

Turner, A. (2000), 'The business case for shared HR services'. IIR Shared HR Services Conference, 28 February.

Ulrich, D. (1995), 'Shared services: from vogue to value', *Human Resource Planning*, **18**, (3).

Workplace Employee Relations Survey (WERS) (1998), Department of Trade and Industry, Essex Univesity Data Archive.

Index